CAMPUS APOCALYPSE

The Student Search Today

CAMPUS APOCALYPSE

The Student
Search
Today

DONALD L. ROGAN

The Seabury Press New York

CONTENTS

1

WHAT ARE STUDENTS TRYING TO DO?

> Speak roughly to your little boy,
> And beat him when he sneezes;
> He only does it to annoy,
> Because he knows it teases.
> *Alice in Wonderland*

I have lived and worked on campus since my own student days twenty years ago. It has always been exciting and rewarding, but in the late 60's it has become a heady way of life—exhilarating, maddening, hilarious, terrifying, beautiful, and tiresome. The college campus, to be trite, has exploded. So many things are going on in so many directions, and at the expense of so many traditions, that no one can feel at a given moment that he is amply aware, let alone on top, of the situation. To have been a college chaplain during these years is to have been, for me at least, almost totally radicalized in theology and in social viewpoint. Something is happening. And it is not only older observers who do not know what it is—the students themselves do not know.

A GENERATION GAP?

Numerous models are currently available for the analysis of student society. According to one model, what we are witnessing is simple *generational rebellion*. Those who are comfortable with this model find it irritating that students generally seem to believe that they are doing new things. Student aberrations, of course, are much easier to handle if they are thought of as a phase. A college trustee who remembers coke and aspirin from his own day might well think that the drug problem is not serious; a parent can misread the demand for coeducational dormitories as merely a more strident means of sowing wild oats. Each adult remembers (and, incidentally, has a lot of unresolved guilt about) his own rebelliousness and is pleased with himself when he can see current student actions as simply more of the same.

For my part, I do not find the model of generational rebellion (or, for God's sake, the "generation gap") very helpful for the purpose of analysis. Built into the model is the hidden expectation that the present unsettledness will all pass, but I no longer think what is happening on the campus is going to phase into the familiar wife and two-and-a-half children in Stamford pattern of the recent past where memory compensated for having sold out for a secure job and a quiet neighborhood. For one thing, many college students today are doing things that will affect their futures in irreversible ways, such as refusing induction into the armed services (or, while in college, planning to) and dealing in illegal drugs. At worst, what is happening will leave scars that will be difficult to hide in suburbia. At best, there may be in the process of being worked out new ground rules for social organization that will make for a lesser distinction between suburbia and the central city. Only time will tell, but the present will not pass without its consequences.

Quite apart from getting black marks on their future employment records, many college students today are staking claim to views which program out the possibility of recanting. You need march on the Pentagon only once for it to be a life-changing experience. For many, it will never be a mere memory; rather, it will shape attitudes which will be quite different from any now observed in America. And the experience is further complicated by the awareness which students have that the attitudes which they are formulating in the American context are also being formulated by students all over the world. A world in which such things take place simply cannot remain the same.

THE MODEL FROM PSYCHOTHERAPY

A second model, one taken from the world of *psychotherapy,* is a refinement of the generational-rebellion model. In this model, students are seen as working through something, shedding the husks of infant and childhood rage and asserting their independence. Campus rebelliousness is basically a manifestation, so the model would indicate, of the identity crisis. There are, of course, still plenty of genuine identity crises on campus as the 60's end. But they seem to me quite different from earlier forms of this crisis in that the students are much more aware today that this is precisely what they are going through. It used to be necessary to apply the label to the case. The case now enters the counselor's office announcing the label himself. This is a phenomenon sufficiently striking to change the character of the ailment entirely. But, even more important, there are now no clear answers to the crisis acceptable to the patient. It is no longer possible to deal with identity crisis vocationally by suggesting direction or purpose to the individual student and assisting him to get down to the business of growing in that direction. Today when he has an identity crisis the student not only knows it, but he also knows that most of the solutions tend to be pat answers, when, in his view, there is simply nothing "out there" for him to attach himself to. But since he does not know who he is or what he is for, finding that something "out there" becomes of overriding importance. He may attempt to solve his problem temporarily by participation in one or more of the kinds of activity available to him on campus, drugs or mysticism or the like. But the model for understanding what he is doing that sees his involvement as therapy for his condition errs if it assumes his critical identity problem is actually being solved. For when the problem exists on the conscious level, its solution is no longer possible in the traditional therapeutic ways. Often he is "into" campus activism or the drug scene precisely because there is no solution to his personal problem. And along the way he may himself realize that there is not going to be any personal solution for him until there is a social solution to many of the problems in the world around him. His activism then becomes a venture taken up for its own sake and not for the purpose of fulfilling himself.

Kenneth Keniston has observed that the organizers of Vietnam Summer (in 1967) were for the most part people whose unconscious identity crisis had occurred earlier in their teens and that the crisis of personality bringing them into participation in activist programs was a second personality crisis. The first crisis "was clearly the major turmoil, guilt, loneliness, anxiety and misery of early adolescence," which led to "a resumption of the preadolescent pattern of success." The second crisis "emerges primarily from the failure of success. Their hesitation may reflect strength rather than weakness. These young men and women usually had already 'proved' that they could succeed in terms that American society uses to define success. Most of them had excelled, but had gained scant satisfaction from their own excellence. So judged, their reluctance to take up the jobs, fellowships, offers and rewards before them might indicate that they were able to demand more, not less of themselves and of life." *

If I read Keniston rightly, students are not "working through" any particular psychological problems when they are as involved and as multidirectional as college students are today, even when their involvement is hostile and anti-Establishment, as much of it quickly becomes. The fact is that they are more assured, more self-conscious, more willing to risk all, than students have ever been in American experience. The model taken from therapy, which suggests that the present turmoil will pass, fails to get at the central facts of most students' motivations. Later I mean to criticize some of their activities as having only therapeutic value, and therefore not worth the evangelism expended on them, but the model under consideration is not the most useful model for understanding what students are doing today.

THE GAME MODEL

Still another model that deserves close and careful attention is the *game model*. This model views the civil rights movement as the game which the students were playing with the South, and with the fascinating organizational and methodological techniques required for that exciting period. As supporting evidence is cited their having left the game when they tired of it and their having then taken up the war game, one with more serious rules and with more at stake. "What would happen if . . . ?" "Let's play like . . ."

* From Kenneth Keniston, *The Young Radicals: Notes on Committed Youth* (New York: Harcourt, Brace & World, 1968), pp. 103–105.

"Suppose the military-industrial complex were vulnerable. How would you go about punching holes in it so that it would deflate?" Once the "name of the game" was clear, the rules wrote themselves. The SDS organization, in its early days, was pure game theory, according to our model, performing the same function that children's games perform, that of teaching techniques and methods of performing tasks that would be of great use later. Carl Oglesby, already gifted at organizational and corporate gamesmanship, found the SDS game more to his liking. In reversing the growth process, he may have ended the gamelike quality of student activism. More likely, as it seems to me, he perceived the utter seriousness of the college game as compared to the trivial commercialism of the corporate game. His choice left a permanent impact on student political thought and work.

But still it might seem essentially gamelike when student life turned to drugs. "Follow the leader," "I dare you," and other child-game commands characterize a great deal of drug activity. And the experiences! Nothing more playful than getting into oneself and finding out the riches there. And this is what drug activity, at the very least, provides: finding out things about yourself you did not know before, what kind of feelings you can have, what kind of things you can see and think, what kind of things you can survive. Although this analysis borders on the macabre, it does successfully explain what students who have been involved with drugs have actually had as motivation and intent. To "climb every mountain" in the essential spirit of youthful conquest was the challenge which, for several years, the availability of drugs laid upon numerous sensitive and aware students. And there was, of course, the added attraction of the game being a secret and illicit one.

The game model could go a long way toward explaining

a great deal of student activity in the current, frenetic period. I refer to it partly in the hope that someone might take it up and make more of it than I can bring myself to do. For me its inadequacy lies in its failure to account for the relentless seriousness of purpose of the college student which has to be recognized, even when, to adults, he is engaged in the most foolish enterprises. Those close to the campus have recognized this seriousness for some time, but now the phenomenon is clear even to those whose knowledge of the campus is dependent on the mass media. The activism that can shut down Columbia University and take on the Chicago Police Department is no longer to be explained as game playing. On the contrary, I would submit that students today are more aware of the actual and theoretical consequences of their actions than students ever have been before. College counselors have long since learned the complete futility of pointing out consequences as a forceful argument against a course of action. A decade ago this would have been explainable as the effect of the Bomb. If, however, this phenomenon of seriousness must be related to the past generation of students and their blaming everything on the Bomb, I would relate the present seriousness as the effect of everyone's having known the horrendous risk to life that the Bomb entailed without having done anything about it. Again, Keniston has his finger on the student pulse when he explains their politicalization in terms of their sense of "nearing the end of the line." For the fact of the matter is that students are not afraid of the Bomb anymore. They are simply fed up that this has become the kind of world that can live with such a fear. And this is not the stuff of which games are made. It is now, as they view the world, a matter of change it or forget it. That some have been willing to press this view into communal living, into common-law marriage and childbearing, is evidence at the least that the seriousness continues to be there. To a large extent this or that aspect of the student scene is playful and gamelike. But the enterprise as a whole is deadly serious and so far, ominously, the only segment of society which seems to realize it are the protectionists who want to stamp it out and have college students go back to panty raids and beach orgies.

THE PARALLEL TO RELIGIOUS EXPERIENCE

In my own analysis I am attracted to a model that is based on *religious experience*. Against the charge that such a choice on my part is obvious, let me hasten to add that I am drearily aware of the talent religious professionals have for hunting down latent religious beliefs in every activity of the human animal, and I deplore it. Daniel Callahan has warned against the "compulsive need of the religious mind to probe beneath the surface of everything for hidden meanings." (Quoted by Harvey Cox in *Commonweal,* Oct. 13, 1967.) This has been much overdone, and if I were to be doing it here I could cease immediately. I do not propose in what follows to baptize the hippies or to find true Christians in the sensitivity-training fad. I do want to suggest that there is viable religious critique of student life and, more importantly, that there is prophetic demand present in what they are doing that challenges the complacency of American religion. But both these are very different tasks from the fad of discerning a religious angle in everything, a fad that has become so prevalent in American pop-theology (in things like *Parables from Peanuts*). Finally, so much of the content of student experimentation and exploration is couched in religious terminology that I am convinced that use of a religious model serves best in meeting students on their own terms.

I also find the religious model instructive because it is by definition provisional and open-ended. The function of a model is both to assist in explaining what is happening and to allow it to continue to happen. The religious model is, if you will, such an incomplete model, and therefore befits the age and incompleteness of the students. It is a model onto which new parts can be fitted as experience and insight demand, yet still a model anchored in recognizable social and individual activity of the past. It is eminently suited to the analysis we are undertaking because it has to do with aspiration and expectation as much as with tradition and dogma. It has also to do at some point with hope.

The particular religious model which I want to employ is one which sees religious experience as fundamentally a search for salvation. Students today are searching for salvation, and they are searching for it with everything in them. They want to be saved—saved from the responsibility of perpetuating the world they see around them, saved from the dreary acceptance of life which they observe about them, and saved from the living death of the adult who rejects his own experience in deference to some authority with power over him. If they could be saved from these prospects, it would be salvation indeed, and the term is not overloaded by so defining it. It is not, of course, "pie in the sky," nor any form of deliverance from danger or risk. It is traditional salvation only if that salvation can be defined within the tradition as "wholeness of personhood" and fulfillment and social health. It will be my thesis here that college students are today venturing upon an extremely serious search for salvation.

THE STUDENT SEARCH FOR SALVATION

The traditional sources of salvation in our society have been the church and, in a less specific sense, the college world itself and the experience of sex. Each of these is explicitly or implicitly rejected today, and it is necessary before proceeding to try to see why.

The primary traditional means of securing salvation, and the one usually thought of as the most important, has been that of accepting and complying with the traditional procedures nurtured and preserved in Christianity around the sacraments of Baptism and the Holy Communion and the experience of the forgiveness of sins with its implicit full participation in a communal church life of fellowship and love. College students, by and large, reject outright this means of salvation. Actually, that rejection has been a long-standing one, although certain ministrations of the church had value on the campus in softening the impact of systematic dehumanization inherent in impersonal structures, especially of large universities. In the past the rejection of the church was usually recanted upon marriage, or at least upon the attainment of parenthood, and the cycle of young adults moving into the congregations of Christendom with sweet memories of liberal college chaplains teaching daring interpretations of doctrine contributed considerable stability to the life of the churches. It even constituted for a time a religious revival. College ministries were altogether beneficial, so it was thought, in developing church members to become intelligent participants. It seems clear today that the rejection taking place during the college years is more permanent than that, partly because it now takes place *before* students come to college and represents also a wholesale rejection of the society which the students are inheriting. The average membership age in all the major churches is rising perceptibly. The church is seen (accurately) as merely one, and the least important one, of the institutions which have been content to continue to make out in a world in which people were in fact living in existential and metaphysical terror. The church's traditional capacity to offer a salvation of sorts (of social sorts, we now know) to college students has disappeared. What we might call the psychological discovery that the church serves as a source of authority for the individual, but at the expense of the integrity of his own capacity for self-authorization, thus at the expense of his individuality, was made long ago, beginning with Freud. It is now an assumption of most intelligent people. And what we might call the sociological discovery that the church serves as a kind of adhesive for society and a safeguard of other social institutions was also made long ago, beginning with Durkheim. This, too, is now an assumption of most intelligent people. Many people can live with these assumptions and still seek, with good conscience, the tenuous individual salvation and social approval of the status quo which the church has to offer, but most college students cannot. They cannot accommodate either the psychological or the sociological explanation, let alone both, to a point where an authentic individualization of faith is a live option for them. The prize, they observe, is hardly worth the effort when it can be sought in so many other places. Such would be the student's analysis of the obvious suggestion that if he is seeking salvation, it is to be found in the church.

SEX AND SALVATION

But what of sex? My generation found its salvation there, and the pursuit of salvation in sex still goes on among students, although it is passing. Up until the present, the modern college student has traditionally accepted a cynical attitude to both the church and the integrity of the educational enterprise, though without particularly acting on either because he has been able to escape into sexual discovery. Sex offered a genuine salvation to generations of students and that it did so is probably the best explanation of why marriage and family eventually tamed them to acceptance of an inadequate society. Sex offered the one opportunity for selfless engagement in a world that was not interested either in love or self-giving. Once the college student progressed beyond the grasping, acquisitive whoring of fraternity legend, there was a girl with whom he found "the meaning of it all." Together they could stand up to anything because the sordid, grasping, acquisitive whoring world could not get at them in their intimacy of spiritual and material I-Thou experience. A surrogate for religious community and a blessed relief from the demands of social consciousness, loving sex experience before and during marriage closed off the vapid nonsalvation of church and college and brought an awareness of community and a sense of wholeness-in-relationship which seemed the answer to all the world's problems. No matter that it was a private solution, and often illicit and therefore secret until marriage —*we* knew what love was and what love the world was still capable of entertaining. The result was lives lived on two levels, a public and a private, but only the private was real. The sexual revolution, imposed, in my judgment, upon the young by the self-justifying imaginations of those who invested a lot in sex and did not find themselves repaid, has ended all that. The result in earlier and more matter of fact sex education has put sex in a different, and perhaps proper, perspective as a biological-psychological, rather than a cosmic-metaphysical, experience. Contraception has, further, made it relatively safe. And no longer is it quite the illicit and secret affair between college men and women that it once had to be. The result is that it is simply not as important as it once was, although this is still only just clearly appearing, and the college generation is still in the turmoil of transition. It is not uncommon today for a coun-

selor to discuss homosexuality with a student who has had
fairly extensive sex experience of both homosexual and
heterosexual kind, and can consequently make comparative
statements which to the counselor himself are merely
academic. Recently I listened to a student's description
of three-way sex activity by himself and his two dates.
His net assessment was that it gave him a great deal to
think about. It is not to condone such behavior to observe
that the mood on sexual subjects is simply different in the
current college student's mind and that his expectation of
finding salvation of any kind in a sphere of life about which
he is so clinical and casual is, to say the least, unlikely.

STUDENT OBJECTIONS TO EDUCATIONAL GOALS

The college itself has been a means of salvation to generations of Americans. Salvation, after all, is at some point a
"way out" of the enervating and lonely life most men lead.
Education has been regarded as salvific in the sense of pre-
senting to the young a chance to deepen their personal
resources of intellect and morale while also preparing them
for marketability in the society at large. It is true that the
liberal-arts tradition in the small colleges upheld the values
that made education function more strenuously than the
multiversity with its mission to society as such, rather
than to the individual, but I will not argue here that the
liberal-arts tradition has succeeded in offering real salvation
where the multiversity has failed. I think in fact it has not.
Students in the large, impersonal universities have a legit-
imate complaint about the quality of student life which
students never experience in the small colleges where the
faculty is accessible to them. But it has been my observation
that salvation is equally withheld from students in the one
setting as in the other. Education itself is simply no longer

capable of offering to students what they regard as salvation, principally because institutions of higher education of whatever type fail to meet the student as student, preferring to think of him as a transient in some stage of preparation. In this sense it makes little difference that the multiversity sees the student in preparation for a career in civil engineering or animal husbandry, while the liberal-arts college regards him as in preparation for "life" (deferring his career preparation to graduate school and thus, in fact, exacerbating the problem)—both regard him as their "product." As the abilities and achievements of college youth improve (and they have, markedly), the continued designation of academic work as preparation for something has been less and less meaningful. Many students today have already experienced achievements that make further preparations for achievement ridiculous. Others sense that life is simply being delayed, or worse, that they are being used by the institutions, if not by the people who run them, for purposes that have nothing to do with themselves at all, but for the gratification of the Establishment. This sense of futility has only been made more grim with the problems presented by the Vietnam war and the awareness that what they are being prepared for, in fact, is reclassification as 1-A and induction into the military service. The debate between the liberal-arts and the multiversity schools is interesting and important, but both fail to communicate the salvation they offer to the students. The students already know, if only by intuition, that what they are being prepared for is otiose, that, in the words of Stanley Kaufmann, "a chief problem for American society has been how to get its best minds to stay in American society and possibly affect it for the better, instead of merely plundering it for enough money to make escape possible" (*New Republic,* Jan. 27, 1968). They cannot be faulted if they choose not to get into

American society to start with, and any way it is looked at, education is the way into American society just as it is the way to escape the status of outsider in that society.

To say that many students reject college as a means of salvation is to say that this *is* the role in which the academic world has cast itself and that the students reject the purpose for which the institution is maintained. This is no longer surprising, now that students seem determined to shut down the institutions which define them, but it remains paradoxical and irrational to many. In its cruder forms, the reaction is that such students should get out of the colleges and make room for those who do accept the purposes of the institution. To hear this simplistic solution and to note the escalating radicalism of entering freshmen each year, is to realize the chasm of understanding which any adequate model for explaining student life must be able to overcome. If the students are seeking salvation, and if the colleges are offering a kind of salvation still plausible to the larger society, why are there problems? Another form of the question that is quite serious is, "Why are students staying in college at all?"

Students might well be, in the future, even more enigmatic than they now are when the logic of this question reaches them. Merely to be enrolled in a college is, to a certain extent, to accept its purposes and to submit to its disciplines. The Free University idea, which allows the students to do education in their own way and for their own purposes, has not yet caught on. I would not be surprised, however, if some of our best young minds did in the future eschew college altogether in favor of doing it themselves, and I shall not be surprised when they succeed. Their honesty should be driving some of them to this already. Meanwhile, why are students in college at all, and in such increasing numbers? The obvious answers are the draft and

vocational necessity. But neither of these is *really* operative
at age eighteen. Two views of college life which are entirely
unconventional and have gained no acceptance with faculty
or administrators are recognizable to students as justification for not dropping out just yet.

College as a puberty rite. It is no longer even necessary
to note that college is a puberty rite for the rich, and
today just about anyone who has not been damaged by
public miseducation beyond a certain point (unfortunately
those who have been so damaged are mostly blacks) can
find himself in college. (It might even be noted that military
service is an alternate puberty rite for the disadvantaged
and a continuation of puberty ritual for the college student,
under the present Selective Service System. Those who still
dare to favor Universal Military Training on the grounds
that it is good for young men to have that experience
would seem to be making this point unreservedly.) College,
in the minds of most college students, is simply a rite which
they are expected to undergo between the ages of seventeen
or eighteen and twenty-one or twenty-two, just as prior
to age seventeen they are supposed to be in elementary and
secondary schools as preparation for this rite. It is foolish
to assert that the large numbers of students in college who
have no idea what they are going to be doing when they
graduate should not be there. In some individual cases, I
am sure it is good that young men go to work or do military
service or something else before going to college, and when
they return find themselves motivated and inner-directed
in a way that most normal collegians simply never experience. But to require that would be to make the colleges
openly pragmatic, and few of them would be willing to see
themselves in this way. Students are in colleges, to be cir-
cular about it, because colleges are there, and it is where
they are supposed to be. Their parents have led them to

believe for years that that is where they would be. Their education up to that point has largely assumed it also. Their friends, over the years, took it for granted, and they themselves expected and "prepared" for it in the sense of assuming that that is what they would be doing. No alternative was ever presented (except military service). Now, any status in life so long anticipated and so generally assumed to be necessary has the character of a rite. Moreover, it is a puberty rite because society expects that when the college years are passed successfully, as indicated by the possession of the undergraduate degree, the young men will then be available for, and, irrationally, prepared for, useful work in the world. Many jobs require a college education without requiring that their holders know, or know how to do, anything that they may have learned in college. Marriage is, it is assumed, deferred until the rite is done, and the rite itself certifies that childhood has been left behind. In a word, leaving college behind is assurance that puberty has been (finally) lived through. This can be the only explanation for society's widespread feeling that the lives of college students should be controlled by the institutions. The phrase that justifies this control is *in loco parentis* (which more than one student has revised to *in loco grandparentis* since they often experience less personal freedom in college than at home). Yet this control is quite different from that exacted by the military over a seventeen-year-old recruit or by an employer over a seventeen-year-old apprentice. The college is expected to exercise a special kind of control over the social and personal (i.e., moral) lives of its students. The rite takes four years, and like all puberty rites is magic in effect.

The student most affected with transferitis, dropout fever, and other February diseases of the college campus responds dramatically to the absurd logic of this reason for his staying in and keeping at it. Such reasoning confirms what he suspects, the absurdity of the entire enterprise. When, on the other hand, he can find no other salvific purpose for being there, even if he is interested in what he is studying, and when he can hardly turn his back on lifelong expectations that this is where he should be at this age, he gains solace from the possibility that even such a purpose might have brought him there.

College as a seemingly necessary place. If my model is correct, it is a fitting place in which to seek salvation. This is true because here one is associated with a large number of peers with whom salvation can be sought and with elders of a slightly different frame of mind than parents or public-school officials, more liberal, less meddlesome, and at first emulated. That the college should be such a place is of first importance to the student, yet this has almost nothing to do with what college administrators think is the purpose of the institution. One might think of education taking place along two parallel tracks in colleges. One of the tracks carries the curriculum, the extracurricular activities of the official college, and the life and work of the faculty. Alongside, neither more nor less related than bare parallelism indicates, is pursued what the student thinks of as his *real* education. This includes his private life, his social life, his extracurricular reading, listening to music, watching films, talking with friends, exploring the meaning of everything around him, and aspiring. It is along this track that he seeks salvation, in his own way, at his own pace, and with his own age group. What goes on along the other track is not completely without interest or importance to him for it assures him that the place for him to live and be and be saved will continue to exist. He may even do assignments with punctuality and creativity, engage in heated and interesting discussions with faculty members, participate in campus government and other college activities (in some kinds of schools he may even be an athlete, although in most schools that is obviously a special category of student), all in order to assure the continued provision of *place* for himself and his friends, who are in reality concerned only with what goes on on the other track. I have tested this analysis out with both faculty colleagues and students, with predictable results. Faculty colleagues think the analysis at best cynical and fundamentally untrue; each can tick off a list of "obviously interested" students. Students generally are either amused to have been found out or in simple agreement.

In the light of this definition of the student's purpose in being in college, it would seem paradoxical that student activism should have turned on the institution itself, except that the essential dishonesty of the institution is beginning to reach the most perceptive in any student body. When students realize that their ideals demand a certain type of community whose purpose is commonly agreed upon, they are then likely to do one of three things: hibernate in order to survive until graduation with as little pain as possible; drop out; or turn on the institution with a fierce challenge to its integrity, including willingness to be violent, if necessary, rather than capitulate to the hypocrisy of it. All that is going on in campus life today falls under one or another of these categories. It may have been observed by many readers already that my description of the college student is a caricature. After all, we are advised, we should not judge the whole generation by the ridiculous actions of a few. I would argue, however, that the power of a minority to extend to other students the alienation which they only may keenly feel is very great; and to assume a process of increasing radicalization among students in the next few years as a result of the activity and experimentation of the minority is not farfetched in the light of the past few years.

We have witnessed this influence in the area of civil rights, where the student with conservative views on the subject is very hard to find today. Moreover, it is my experience that most students are far more similar to each other than any are to me or other of their elders, that not very far beneath the surface of any of them is a seething impatience that is not generational, not merely functional and not a game, and that rejects the traditional means of seeking and finding salvation. After Chicago, 1968, students who would not think of themselves as radical at all found themselves in almost absolute sympathy with "The Movement." I fell into the trap of judging a particular student to be an authentic conservative because he had been so described to me by other students. On the surface he seemed the perfect model of those who would say that there is nothing to the student revolution. Excellent grades. Neat, trim appearance. Polite manner. Frequent discussion in support of his college's administration. Not part of the drug scene. Some matter or other brought us together and a few minutes conversation proved to me that though his fellow students might find him on the opposite side of some battles, he was far more alienated from the college establishment than many others I knew. He agreed enthusiastically with my analysis of education proceeding on two tracks, one for the faculty and another for the student. He had performed extremely well (and easily) on the faculty track simply to keep them off his back.

Let me be quite clear. The salvation of college students, as of all men, might very well be found in church or in sex or in college or in many other structures of human experience and community. My point is that the college student no longer seeks salvation in any of these, but is nonetheless seeking it in many other kinds of activity; that in fact the proper model for explaining what is going on among college students today is the religious model of the search for salvation, even though the search is not pursued in any of these areas where men have thought salvation to be available.

2

THE LURE OF DRUGS

The campus behavior most bewildering and most threatening to society is that associated with drug use. I would argue, on the strength of the religious model, that a good portion of drug abuse among college students can be explained as arising from the student's search for salvation. The model will also serve to explain the limitations encountered in the use of this means and its passing. For drugs as vehicles of salvation, it seems clear, are no longer very widely sought after, although, many unintended results from continued drug use for other reasons have survived.

Marijuana and Hallucinogenic Drugs

At the outset, it is necessary to differentiate the use of marijuana from that of hallucinogenic drugs. Perhaps in the early days of its use on campus, marijuana was justified as helpful in securing a kind of genial camaraderie that contrasted starkly with the competitiveness of life in general and constituted a saving escape from reality. Certainly the mystique of *nouveau* marijuana use, with its controlled environment and rituals of manipulation, had suggestive overtones of sacramental worship. But the day is long since past when marijuana had for college students the same

22

importance as those primitive rituals required. It is still widely used and widely available, both on and off campus, and so widely available that controlling the source in any one community is virtually impossible; but, somewhat as with sex, it now tends to be taken for granted and accepted as a part of life—in some cases a part of each individual's day—rather than accorded a salvific role. Marijuana was a fad and, like all fads, manifested religious overtones at a given point. At present it is simply a phenomenon, too common to bear any special significance, except as a factor in the breakdown between various classes in society.

Furthermore, marijuana is not primarily a student drug, since it had been widely used in the ghettos long before students knew about it and has moved down on the age scale into lower-level educational institutions and out on the social scale into the middle class. In both areas it may be a more serious index of social change than it ever has been on the campus, but at least its extensive use off the campus makes it something less than a special student issue. Not to separate marijuana from other drugs in discussing the drug phenomenon as an aspect of students' lives is to refuse to talk about students as they actually are. Invariably, in a counselor's conversation with students about drugs, the student will say, "Of course, I don't mean marijuana."

The larger society may be more troubled by our differentiating, for analysis, marijuana from other drugs than by any other aspect of our discussion. The widely accepted domino theory of drug use assumes that marijuana is but the first step into an underworld of illicit temptations over the later stages of which the individual no longer has any control. No responsible studies of drug use in contemporary American society give support to the theory that marijuana is the introduction to a series of steps leading to irreversible heroin addiction. The correlation is simply not present in the statistical information about drug use. It is generally estimated (with wide geographical variations) that better than half of all college students have smoked marijuana at one time or another, many of them on several occasions. Statistics on hallucinogenic drug use or addictive narcotics include far fewer students. The student's insistence that marijuana is different has some substance for close observers of college drug use. As with the domino theory, which once supported the Vietnam war, it is true that dominoes will fall in a certain way if they have been set up to do so. The legal situation which lumps together the vast number of pot smokers in this country with all other drug users as felons has created a situation in which respect for the integrity of the law has been the chief casualty. The danger resulting from legal prohibitions of use or possession of marijuana, together with attendant social disintegration produced by illegality, is the only established danger found in marijuana use. This is a serious danger indeed, and it is not to say that other dangers might not be established with more systematic study than the social panic of the past has allowed. But such danger to the individual as marijuana is now known to present, it would seem, is the result of a situation that has been created by society, not by the drug.

THE GENESIS OF THE DRUG PROBLEM ON CAMPUS

No one, in fact, can justify complete surprise that drug use finally exploded into an American campus problem. For American society itself has been drug oriented in that it has assumed without serious questioning that the instant relief of pain or tension to be found in pharmaceutical preparations is a value to be sought. This fact goes hand in hand with the observation of Helen H. Nowlis that American

society is one "dedicated to progress through chemistry." *
The sordid story of controls on patent medicines available
to the public without medical supervision is sufficient testi-
mony to the irresponsibility of the larger society on the
whole question of what kind of compounds can justifiably
be sought and enjoyed as a benefit of chemical technology.
And the practice of seeking mood changes by ingestion of
substances constitutes a real illusion of the availability of
"salvation" to all who grow up in this society. If it is true
that the basic factor in all drug abuse is the availability of
drugs to abuse, then the favorable attitude toward drugs and
their use provided by our culture is certainly strongly to
blame for the drug problem. This approving attitude seems
to warrant, at first sight, the right to make use of whatever
is physically available, unwise as the adventure might eventually prove to be. The society only confirms the reality of
this charge laid upon it when it seeks a scapegoat in the
student with his apparent obliviousness to the nice distinction between the legal and the illegal.

A full analysis of marijuana use in this country is still
lacking, and indeed use of it may already be so widespread
as to make such an analysis impossible or irrelevant. My
point is that it is not primarily a campus problem and is not
used in what I think of as the students' search for salvation.

In concentrating on the hallucinogens, I am also omitting
any consideration of the more specifically medical problems
arising from the use by students of amphetamines and
barbiturates, and from the indiscriminate use of "Speed"
(methaphetamine), which is a serious danger to some
students. In general, student use of these drugs is for prag-

---

* *Drugs on the College Campus* (A Guide for College Administrators). A publication of the Drug Education Project of the National Association of Student Personnel Administrators, under Contract FDA
67-3, Food and Drug Administration, December, 1967.

matic purposes and is not a particularly new occurrence. The drugs in this category most commonly used are stimulants that combat fatigue and sleepiness, to which students turn in times of academic stress and pressure. The literature on the subject offers evidence that their use, both prescribed and unprescribed, in society in general, is also a serious problem, and the conclusion can be drawn that in the use of these drugs, student culture is imitative rather than inventive.

THE HALLUCINOGENS IN A SALVATION CONTEXT

The hallucinogens are another story, for their use has produced a particular lore among their defenders which quite clearly relates them to the search for salvation. Emanating from campus centers, a whole "psychedelic" subculture has permeated the American scene, affirming the expansion of the individual consciousness as the solution to the problems of living in an ambiguous and hostile world. Unfortunately the adjective "psychedelic" has been commercially used to describe such a large variety of items that definition of it would be quite useless at this stage, but it was first applied to LSD (d-lysergic acid diethylamide, "acid"), mescalin, psilocybin, and other drugs to characterize their effects, chiefly the infinite enlargement of the visual capacity and the proliferation of perceptual acuity. Although the properties of these drugs differ in intensity and manner of effect, they are sufficiently similar in some respects to warrant their religious value to the user.

LSD has been most sanely studied by Sidney Cohen, M.D., in *The Beyond Within,* and any deficiencies in the present discussion should be corrected by close study of that excellent book. It is clear from his study, from the literature generally, and from my own observations made in counseling students on the subject of drug use, that a religious framework of reference in describing the effects of hallucinogens arises with striking frequency in reporting the experience. This, to be sure, has been the contention of Timothy Leary for many years, although his gratuitous invention of a religious society to justify and escape punishment for his own violations of drug laws seems suspect to most observers—an exploitation of the American sentimentality about religion whereby anything done in its name is permissible, a fact of religious life in this country that ought to be attacked on many fronts.

Students who speak of finding religious experience in drug use emphasize, as the chief marks of that experience, the new and unforetold self-knowledge, the unsuspected sense of the presence of the divine, and above all an overwhelming conviction of unity. Whether he has merely heard of these effects from other users and is seeking the experience on their authority, or whether he is interpreting his own experience in such terms in retrospect, and thus pursues the experience further in additional uses of the drug, the student is clearly seeking or believing himself to be finding a salvation experience in hallucinogenic drug use. At the very least, it should be possible to recognize this, to resist the temptation to label it a rationalization for activity that we think is in reality just for "kicks," and to note the implicit challenge to traditional religious experience presented in the student's report. For remarkable to the user and important to his view of the drugs as a special means of salvation is the fact that the experience is different from that offered to him by traditional religious means. It may be that what the drug user thinks he achieves in the drug experience is not, and cannot be, available to him in conventional religious experience, but his search for it is not dishonorable merely for that reason.

genic drug experience and religious experience would in-
A closer look at the relationship between the hallucino-
dicate that there can be little doubt that what occurs has a
character usually described as religious. William Braden, in
The Private Sea: LSD and the Search for God, sought as
full an analysis of this relationship as possible on the
grounds that it should be given benefit of doubt at a time
such as this when so much of conventional religious thought
was under re-examination. Although I think he sometimes
oversimplifies, his description of the religious aspect of the
LSD phenomenon is close to that commonly given by the
users themselves. The elements of the experience are the loss
of the sense of self and personal ego, the loss of the sense of
time, the loss of confidence in the meaning of words, the
disappearance of duality, and the rising confidence that one
knows all there is to know; and Braden is right in equating
these with the general descriptions of mystical experience.
It goes without saying that this experience can be terrifying
to the individual unprepared for it and, indeed, even with
preparation, such instant mysticism is not for everyone.

We might also call attention to two instances of the use of
hallucinogenic drugs as a means of acquiring religious insight and experience. The first instance is the practice in the
Native American Church of using in their services a mush-
room with hallucinogenic properties. Because of this practice the church has been regularly summoned before state
courts; the antiquity of the practice is generally advanced
as an argument in its favor. Nevertheless, some states have
outlawed the use of drugs in religious worship, and their
action is not dissimilar to that of the State of Arkansas,
which a few years ago outlawed the serving of alcoholic
beverages to minors, specifically including the serving of
communion wine in church ceremonies. Both cases are
indicative of the vulnerability of American legal concepts

when confronted with authentic religious practices. The second instance was Timothy Leary's attempt to show, in the widely discussed "Good Friday experiment," that the religious experiences on that holy day of theological students who had ingested LSD and of a control group that had been given a placebo were essentially indistinguishable, the insights, perceptions, and aspirations of both groups being the same. His conclusion was that LSD induced religious experience of an authentic kind as effectively as more traditional disciplines of religious devotion.

In his book, Cohen correctly observes that our scientific understanding of religious experience has been unnecessarily impeded by wrong-headed values and that such values help to produce the ambivalence any observer might feel about the claims of religious experience in drug use. Attempting a preliminary analysis, he suggests as a possible definition of religious experience the "dyssynchrony of the reticular formation of the brain" and asks, "Does this lessen its [the experience's] value to the individual and his society?" Some adequate definition would seem, in fact, to be the only hope for sensible analysis of the chemically induced experience under LSD to be able to make close comparison of it with equally clinical analysis of more traditional experience. Refocusing the visionary experience from the less empirical version of an observer like Braden, Cohen notes that "very substantial alterations of the ego" are common to religious experience, in which two psychological processes are evident: "a marked reduction in the critical faculty" and an alteration in "the usual manner of processing incoming data." These work hand in hand to bring to the notice of the subject objects and scenes that would normally be routinely screened out from observation and allow him to evaluate them in ways different from his day-to-day manipulation of environment. In traditional religious experience, such states are brought about as the distant result of arduous and lengthy disciplines of self-control and, as the old manuals used to call it, "mortification." That they were carefully cultivated habits, taken up for motivations arising from the desire for sanctity, in no sense removes them from empirical observation. And when they are isolated for analysis, it can be seen, as Cohen observes, that the chemical inducement of the same states is hardly surprising.

When a college student who never goes to church and seems to have no interest in the disciplines or devotions of the religious community in which he grew up describes a drug experience as if it were a vision into the divine, in which he has seen things more clearly than ever before and values them differently than he had prior to the experience, he is not necessarily making up the story to justify his behavior by an appeal to the most respectable of categories, the religious. The fact may well be that exactly the same things have been happening to his personality as happen in religiously disciplined experience. It may also be the case, such is American religious practice, that he had never witnessed firsthand an authentic religious experience in his family church. An important, but distracting, philosophical point is that in neither case does the experience itself justify the rational assertion that the divine thus encountered has objective reality. If such an observation is made to the tripping student, it must also be made to the ecstatic monk or the fervent worshiper in the pew.

Secondary characteristics clearly essential to religious experience also seem to obtain in a "good trip" and in the kind of religious exploration the acid user seeks. They include the preliminary expectation that the state of being which he seeks is available, a sort of predisposition to this kind of "faith"; environmental congeniality; and the assistance of others, more experienced in the phenomenon, who will "guide" and interpret the perceptions of the experience in the right direction. That such secondary characteristics developed and were used quite naturally in the early experience with LSD on campuses suggests a kind of inchoate religious sense attaching itself to the drug scene.

There are tertiary characteristics also. For example, the kind of hopes expressed when the chief argument for the use of LSD and hallucinogenics in general was their religious value tended to be messianic in character. That is to say, all virtue was invested in the substance as the cure for all the world's ills. Irresponsible talk about "turning on" Lyndon Johnson to end the Vietnam war and dangerous actions like the now famous "turning on" of the Hell's Angels, indicated that nothing short of the messianic age was to be expected once such depth of individual experience as the trip provided was known by all men. Any counselor knows dangerous and sometimes tragic cases of a genial acidhead giving LSD to another person without his knowledge in the confidence that nothing but good could come of it. The "reduction in the critical faculty" had its extremes, as all religious phenomena do.

THE COMMUNAL ELEMENT

The communal element in hallucinogenic drug use proved, also, to be epiphenomenal. There was a time when, as we have noted, the user could count on there being a community of concern, bound together partly by their panic of the outside world and within which the creed of acid hope could be fervently embraced. The nature of the experience, however, made that an impossible ideal, for the experience is essentially individual in two senses. First, the user's own perceptions are altered so dramatically that he sees and experiences things he has never seen before. An experienced guide can recognize the symptoms of various stages of the trip, but only the user himself sees what he is seeing, although others can respond in some form of "Sure you did" to what he says he saw. Whatever bonds of relationship might be established among people who have the same *kind* of experience, the extreme individuality of the experience is bound to have its toll. The touchstone of genuine religious experience has always been the sense of community possessed by the individual and shared in empirically testable ways with others, but this test has never been possible in the case of experiences that are entirely inward in character. Salvation is more than simply having experiences. Another element in the experience isolating the individual and militating against any communal sharing in the religious sense is the virtually total unpredictability of the particular effects that the drug will have on the user. No amount of preliminary suggestion can assure that an individual's experience with the drug will be satisfactory in any given respect, let alone the religious experience encountered. There are too many variables. According to Helen H. Nowlis, "One thing is known with certainty [about drugs in general]: there are no direct, simple, reliable cause and effect relationships between any drug and any behavior."

The writer also had the opportunity to observe closely what happened when the drug known popularly as "MDA" was first introduced. Student users were confidently told by other students that the drug had none of the religious limitations of other hallucinogenic drugs, and its secondary and tertiary characteristics seemed to assure all observers that a new phenomenon was present. Although the precise character of MDA was unknown on the occasion when I first saw its effects, it did produce a mild hallucinogenic effect in which the user saw not objects in the room around him, not the unity of all things in the divine unity, but *other people,* and saw them as if for the first time. Warm human relationships were deeply felt between people who had had little but passing acquaintance with each other. Intensity of concern for one another characterized all the participants. The barriers that normally divide people and categorize relationships seemed to be broken down.

As word spread of the effects of this drug—it was first used among relatively few people—nothing ill could be said about it, and indeed, no ill effects other than social divisiveness between those who had and those who had not used it ever developed in any but one or two of the participants. Having been for some time close to the drug scene, I was astounded at the numbers and types of people who were swayed by evangelism in behalf of this drug; but after the first wave of enthusiasm fed into a second, the members of the older drug scene, for the most part, disassociated themselves from it entirely for fear that the openness and expansive congeniality of its users would result in a social disaster, such as a bust. No attempts to persuade or influence individuals succeeded in bringing it under control, and it quickly became apparent that where "salvation" was so clearly available at the simple drop of a cap(sule), nothing but the strictest authority could even meet the situation. In time the event passed into memory, but student after student still extolled the virtues of the drug itself and claimed new capacities for charity in himself as a result of its power over him. An index of its hopefulness was that many students confided to me that it was a drug to end drugs, since it gave an entirely new perspective on the people with whom one associated, including faculty and administrators, and consequently it was motivating everyone to buckle down to serious academic work as an earnest of their new-found brotherhood with all mankind. This, of course, did not happen.

The net result of the search for salvation by use of MDA was the pathetic despair that eventually ensued among those who had been given a chemical glance into what life could be, the experience defining for them life's boundaries, requirements, and possibilities, with a genial vagueness almost criminal in its misleading effect on them. The search for salvation had failed, just on the verge of its success.

It will remain a question whether the search for salvation ought ever to arrive at its goal, or whether the meaning of the search is not in the search itself. With drugs it seems clear that one of the religious deficiencies of the chemical search for salvation is that a violent and embarrassing anticlimax of aftereffect eventually sets in, that each discovery becomes one more penultimate instead of the ultimate. But the question we ought to ask ourselves is: In what terms have we so falsely but effectively characterized the religious quest as to lead the young to expect that its completion is quickly to be found when the right key is turned up? The great amount of religious language present in reports of trips indicates, at the least, a great religious void in the college student's life and the inadequacy of his religious training. The content of hallucinations is the result of suggestibility in the environment and in the personality of the subject. It seems that religion was on the minds of drug users in very challenging ways.

The Negative Factors in Drug Experience

Despite the obvious connections between religious experience, particularly mysticism, and the hallucinogenic drug experience, I would assert that the search for *salvation* in drugs has largely been abandoned by college students. Such is the case with drugs (as with alcohol and cigarettes as well) that drug abuse will be with us for some time to

come, and the social panic it breeds will continue with
equal vigor to prevent much useful research from taking
place and producing the extensive information needed about
the precise usefulness of the hallucinogenic drugs. In what
follows I want to comment on the disillusionment with
drugs which has resulted in the religious dimension of drug
use becoming less important, without offering any false
confidence that drug use will not continue to be a serious
social problem.

The real difficulty, it seems to me, with any hopeful
search for a chemical salvation lies in the twofold character
of bodily chemistry as individual and impersonal. What
takes place in drug experience as we have already noted, is
essentially individualized behavior, an experience solely
within the confines of an individual's own system. Effects
of the same drug may be simultaneously felt by others
around him, but the primary source of effect on the individual user will be from within himself, not from those around
him. The essential communal awareness in drug experience
is at best temporary, and in fact it is usually a function of
extraneous factors such as the necessity of like associating
with like at a time such as our own when drug use is so
offensive to large parts of society. Paradoxically, the more
widespread drug culture becomes, the less communal can it
be. Drug life then is a kind of world-within-a-world with no
real capacity to meet the problems of the world outside.

Drug experience, it must be emphasized, is impersonal,
despite the impression some users have to the contrary.
Only that can be personal which fully defines the person;
consequently, that which is possible and present to oneself
alone, even with the help of a physical, chemical substance,
is only potentially or partially personal. Interaction with
other people is required for full human personhood, but
not for hallucinations. To know oneself in all the fantastic

variety of possibilities which the human system presents is necessary, but it is not the final necessity: the final necessity is to know others.

THE THERAPEUTIC USE OF DRUGS

Another way of putting this is that drug use may well be therapeutically valuable. The religious model of the search for salvation explains a good deal of the motivation behind drug use among college students, but the therapeutic model alone seems able to explain why the search is misguided. Cohen observes that not only religious experience and hallucinogenic drug use require "patient hopefulness, proper setting and therapist conviction"—the primary factors noted above. These also "are necessary prerequisites for all successful psychotherapies." The implication is that at a crucial point psychedelic drugs require both the religious and the therapeutic model for full understanding. So the point that the writer would emphasize is that while the therapeutic model may at this stage prove more useful than the religious model in explaining student drug use, nonetheless where therapy is necessary, salvation is not (yet) possible.

Thus it may be useful, and even necessary, in arriving at a full understanding of what it is to be human to secure an understanding of humanity's past. This is the psychedelic (as it is the McLuhanite) discovery of man's capacity for holistic perception and for the full interplay of body and mind. Also, it may be desperately necessary for each man to arrive at a full understanding of his individual past. This is the psychedelic and psychoanalytic therapy derived from the shift in perceptual orientation. But these must be seen *as* culturally and individually therapeutic. The search for salvation lies beyond successful therapy. The point is that the chemical interactions which produce an expanding of consciousness are but a variation on the full and adequate definition of the human being; they are, we could say, already present by definition in humanity. Continuing variations on the theme might be interesting, but they are not salvific since they require ignoring the problem presented by other people. There is infinite possibility of exploration in the hallucinogenic experience, exploration that may or may not be available in other ways. It has not been proven that there is growth.

Drugs and the Law

A different sort of barrier (and problem) against salvation-by-drugs is the societal resistance to nonmedical drug ingestion as represented in the drug laws. The student word for the unending and unproductive difficulty of dealing with opposition on this point is "hassle." Drug use threatens the larger society immensely, but this threat has only temporary significance for the student, for it exposes a wound—the guilt which society has about its own sanctioned drug abuse—but nothing more is accomplished. In the eyes of the student, acid is not worth dying for, since that would be the end of the very experience which defines its value. There may still be students venturing into hallucinogen experimentation in their individual search for salvation, but there are fewer and fewer veterans of the search who will give them much encouragement.

An Evaluation of the Drug Experience

Three observations remain to be made about the period in which drug abuse seemed to beckon with saving power. The first is that students with hallucinogenic experience did unveil, in striking ways, the mysteries of the mind, of perception, for themselves and for the rest of us. The full knowledge of man, and the comparatively blasphemous non-use of human resources, now has dimensions known previously only psychiatrically (and, I would add, in past religious disciplines). Society is not organized to recognize the fullness of humanity, and most individuals in society are ill equipped to handle the insights into themselves which acidheads have known. The society is still predominantly linear and rational; too few categories of experience are commonly available for understanding the full gamut of man's experience. A glimpse into some of the possibilities has been provided by psychedelic drugs. This is now a world in possession of "The Yellow Submarine," and I am not prepared to say that our prepsychedelic world was quite complete without it. It is now necessary to plunge more seriously and systematically into the conscientious study of man in his wholeness—a project our departmentalized institutions of higher education are not capable of doing. The search for salvation cannot be serious until such study becomes normal.

The second observation is that society must boldly confront the challenge offered by the many students who have come through their hallucinogenic experiences relatively unscathed. Of what value are the generalizations about the dangers of drug use when contradictory evidence has presented itself to us regularly? This point, it seems to me, speaks to the social panic that LSD generated, and it serves as an example of the futility of panic in the face of problematical situations. Had drug use been seen in time as a kind of search for salvation rather than assumed to be demonic and conspiratorial of traditional values, a more balanced attitude toward the phenomenon might have been possible. As a result of our panic a different kind of wound has been exposed and remains exposed by those who have tripped, some many times, without harm and possibly with real help to themselves in a therapeutic sense—the wound of uncertainty about the values thought threatened. Civilization is undoubtedly a delicate instrument, easily destroyed. But it seems equally clear that frenzied efforts to protect it accomplish little beyond the ego satisfaction of the defenders.

The third observation arises from the tragedy of those who have not come through psychedelic drug experience unscathed, or more, those who still are involved with drug experimentation for reasons that are various and often ridiculous but which add up to a kind of spiritual masturbation, a turning in on the self with infinite fascination and the implicit rejection of hope for the real world. There is refuse left behind whenever the search for salvation fails. If the college students are seeking to define the world as a place in which "beautiful" things happen, and therefore a place where they ought to be made to happen in so far as possible, they must also realize that the world is a place where very sad things happen that neither foresight nor enthusiasm can prevent. Sidney Cohen ends his study of LSD on such a sad note: "The tragi-comedy that is the story of a quarter century of LSD is not yet over. A final melancholy act is still to be played. It will be years before the curtain falls upon the psychedelic scene. The present cast will have to leave the stage before a more hopeful, new beginning can commence." *

There are a good many college students who have had extensive drug experience and who once invested hallucinogens with religious importance, and who have now left drugs behind. ("Of course, when I say drugs, I don't mean marijuana.") A radical student leader from Princeton is thus quoted, "I don't have anything against drugs, but they

* *The Beyond Within* (New York: Atheneum, 1964), p. 288.

just sidestep the issue." (*Newsweek*, March 17, 1969) Another student put it this way: "If you take the pill, then chemically you are *forced* to look freely at yourself. It is as if we no longer have it within ourselves to reach out and touch the terrible truths, as if we haven't the faith and the guts to get us there on our own. Where is America's confidence? The confidence that doesn't depend on pills and degrees and sunglasses, on the new look and the club card, and approval of the authority. Have our governments and schools done so much for us that we have completely forgotten that we can do some things on our own?" *

The failure of the search for salvation in psychedelic drugs need not mean, and for the best students does not mean, the end of the search. Students who have left drugs behind have done so to go on to other things.

It is important to point out that this does not mean that society has won any battle in its war with college students. The contemptible myopia of the drug laws can still rouse a student's ire. But drugs themselves are not the issue, and students interested in their search for salvation are increasingly regarding drugs as a drag on the real search. Many have discovered that people-people exploration has more potential than people-chemical exploration.

* *To Make a Difference: A Student Look at America,* ed. Otto Butz (New York: Harper & Row, 1967), p. 20. Used with permission.

3

THE PROMISE SOUGHT IN SENSITIVITY TRAINING

Many students have discovered an answer to their own intuitions of the insensitivity of the society around them in what is known loosely as sensitivity training. They have quickly invested it with sufficient importance so that we can readily discern in it another facet of their search for salvation. The student's initial encounter with sensitivity experience evokes in him both the sense of panacea and evangelistic zeal that characterize religious discovery. And the redress found for the student's most severe problem, the gap between what people say and what people actually are, is assurance that a saving experience has been turned up. The effect of hallucinogenic drugs on perception includes for many subjects a kind of insight into the self that, for the first time, opens up to the individual the depths and variety of awareness of which his personality is capable. But it has generally been difficult, to say the least, to make any use of the insight because of the intense privacy of the experience. Sensitivity work, on the other hand, seems to accomplish much the same thing in a context where human relationships are central to its application. The student enters upon sensitivity training programs because there he learns from others the possibility of his becoming a better person; and the observation should not be passed over lightly that this is precisely what he wants to be and that he regards this, in his enthusiasm, as the key to his salvation.

THE STUDENT DESIRE FOR SENSITIVITY

Sensitivity, when achieved, is not unkind, and consequently it is not precisely accurate to attribute the student's desire for this quality to his feeling that the world in which he lives is managed by people of remarkable insensitivity. Yet any search for salvation arises, of necessity, out of a consciousness of lostness and "damnation," which, in the case of the college-age youth, takes the form of his never having the sense of being treated as a person. Rather, it seems to him, he is an instrument serving some purpose suitable to others than himself. This results, inevitably, from the psychology of growth which requires that every entry upon a new threshold of experience be authenticated as fully as possible by an overwhelming sense of its newness and freshness. No couple are really "in love" unless they are convinced that they are the first couple who have ever been. No vocation to service is firmly fixed until it dawns on the subject that no one has ever quite done that particular job before. No poem is written without the assurance that nothing like it has ever appeared before.

Growth, however, brings with it a broadening in the experiencing of life as well as a deepening of that experience, and it is this broadening that harbors a negative aspect. For real growth is also inevitably accompanied by an awareness that not only others have preceded one along the way but also they have failed to give any adequate indication either of the pain involved in moving forward or the delights to be encountered. To the young person the former seems intolerable, the latter incredible; and the only conclusion to be drawn is that these forerunners are insensitive and using "me" for their own purposes. Parents are so seen by their children, teachers by their students, recruits by their drill instructors, doctors by their patients. The theological term for this is original sin, pointing to the painful loneliness of the individual in his growth period, made more painful as he discovers the lack of originality in his progress. Thus the pattern of growth of which the college student is so intensely aware very nearly requires that he fail to find any indication in the world in which he lives that he is thought of as a person in his own right.

This conviction also receives confirmation from his educational experience prior to college. In his eyes the egocentricity of all educational activity is perverse. All his life he has found himself the center of attention and treated both as the recipient of some kind of gift and the subject of complicated organization and manipulation—all presumably for his sake. Yet from his side it appears that all this attention has really been for somebody else's sake, and the mystery of all giving relationships comes home to him when, at some unpredictable moment in his educational career, he yields to the temptation to refuse the gift in order to see what will happen. The process continues as if, on his part, there had been no withdrawal! He then knows that he has successfully exposed the flaw in our educational theory, that truth cannot be a gift from one to another, and in so doing has confirmed for himself that those who are involved in administering his education are doing so for their own purposes and not for any value he may have to them.

When he arrives at college, he expects something different, for he has now joined a community of scholars. Instead, he finds himself regarded once more as preparing for some future state rather than yet fully alive. Moreover, in most institutions of higher education, even liberal-arts colleges, he is, as he sees it, of only functional importance to his teachers: the only relationship they are willing to have with him is academic. No matter how free and generous they may be with their time to discuss a term paper or test, or to give him additional help in his work, it is solely about his academic work that he feels them related to him and himself to them. He senses further that when the faculty member talks to his colleagues, there is even a different tone of voice and vocabulary than when he talks to students. The credibility gap, the insensitivity pattern, thus is found at the center of a life which is described as communal and to that degree falsely labeled. He is not a person to his teachers, far less to the administrators of his institution, and so he proceeds to pursue his real education on that private track that we have already described. Along that track, eventually, he will find the opportunity for sensitivity training as a corrective for all of this. Alas, by that time he will have left most of his teachers far behind, in his own estimation, as unredeemable.

(In defense of the teacher, since I do not in this chapter want to be insensitive: Students, like the rest of us, view the world as that organization of reality which exists where they are. While in college, that is the world. When on vacation, that is the world. When graduated, where they then find themselves is the world. The insensitivity of students, often, is their failure to realize that the faculty member lives in the college, that even when it is not in session, it is still his world in some sense. And when the student graduates, the college is still the world for the faculty member. The longer he survives in his world, the more transient do students become as individual beings. He has been forgotten often enough to assume that he will be forgotten again. When he is proved right, he too has the sense of not being regarded as a person. So much, however, for such a defense. It seems clear to me that the improvement the situation requires is more within the power of the teacher to bring about than of the student.)

Students are interested in sensitivity training, then, because it provides such a marked contrast with the limitations of the classroom and lecture hall, where, no matter how sliced, what they say and what they feel is not important. This constitutes a search for salvation in sensitivity experience insofar as such adventures seem capable of being translated back into the real world sufficiently to change it, and in the hope that the world where his future is being dealt with and the world where he is a real person can somehow be brought together. It is with immense hopefulness that students go into this activity, as it is of consequence that they quickly forget the problem of the insensitivity of others in the discovery of their own. The activity assists them in overcoming insensitivity in themselves.

The meaning of "sensitivity" in student parlance is openness to feelings. It is not an anti-intellectual concept, but it is nonintellectual. It depends on the observation that experience is a teacher itself and that an academic curriculum allows all too little room for experience and its necessary interpretation, that communication involves a good deal more than words. It is, then, the translation of a therapist's talents for perception of nonverbal interchange by which alone he can discern the full meaning of the self before him. To increase one's own sensitivity is to become better able to perceive what is being said underneath the words used by others, and to be in the presence of sensitive people is to be assured that one's own feelings are being compassionately read and received.

THE TRAINING PROCESS

"Sensitivity training" is a term applied to a large variety of techniques developed for numerous purposes but primarily in the interests of research into the functioning of individuals in groups. It has in recent years been popularized to a sufficient extent for factionalism to have appeared and for infinite variations on the techniques to have developed. Its origins are in group therapy but its appeal lies in the fact that emotional states and their effect on human relationships are so complex that all of us are in need of a little bit of therapy. Undoubtedly charlatans and novices have misused the techniques developed by professional psychologists, but this is a sad eventuality affecting any successful human resource. I am not sure that, for most people, the faddish bastardizations of sensitivity training are all that dangerous. We are all involved in manipulating others all the time through our insensitivity. It is difficult to see why conscious manipulation is any more dangerous than social life itself. My resource in what follows is the practice of sensitivity training as it reaches the college student, tutored by an informal publication entitled "Reading Book, Twenty-First Annual Laboratories in Human Relations Training, 1967–68," which bears the authority of the Institute for Applied Behavioral Science associated with the National Education Association (NEA), Washington, D.C. My additional resource is two decades of familiarity with the use of sensitivity techniques in church life.

Beginning in 1947, the National Training Laboratory (NTL) has systematically pursued research in human relations with the sponsorship of the Research Center for Group Dynamics (now at the University of Michigan) and the NEA. In the past decade, NTL has been active in applying its techniques of sensitivity training in various occupational fields. There are now regional centers across the country and a recognizable "establishment" in the field. The broad purpose of sensitivity training may be stated as remedial education in the art of being human. Its remedial aspect is, of course, a commentary on educational life in America and its optimism arises out of the belief that human errors in the educational process can be factored out. Its overall purposes would be accomplished if the educational system could absorb its techniques (without neglecting its theory), if teachers and administrators in the educational structure could be "sensitized" and children allowed to progress in sensitivity instead of what they now accomplish in the inhuman operation of our educational systems, which is to progress in an adept defensiveness, effectively shutting out others from their real selves and bottling up within themselves talents for relationship which would make any adult venture more virtuous. Should the school system succeed in sensitivity training at every level, remedial work with college students and adults would, presumably, not be necessary. This is a counsel of perfection, of course, and has value only in so far as it clearly focuses on the purpose of sensitivity training by imagining it successful.

An introductory course in psychology at the University of Michigan includes, as the laboratory portion of its offering, a spectrum of activities called Project Outreach, "an attempt to define and describe a number of areas that are directly connected with psychology, which are the subject of ongoing psychological inquiry, and which supplement the subjects studied in the more abstract classroom situations with actual real-life work or participation experiences in a way that enhances both academic understanding and personal development." (Quoted from a mimeographed course handout.) The laboratory is "the laboratory of everyday living" and the program includes work projects in mental health, law, conflict, civil rights, cultural enrichment and educational reform as well as "group process" which is, of course, the sensitivity training item in the course.

T-GROUP LAB WORK

Students who sign up for "T-Group" lab work (the meaning of "T" in T-Group is the subject of amiable joking in the profession in that rather than "training" it can easily also turn out to stand for "tyranny") are offered as objectives an increase in "self-insight," better understanding of other persons, awareness of one's impact on others, a better understanding of procedures occurring within groups and increased skill in working in a group setting (*ibid.,* cf also "Reading Book," p. 2). In groups of ten to fifteen people, including two trainers, participants are faced with a totally unstructured and apparently purposeless group which they must develop into a social organization, out of the compulsion to arrive at some social *raison d'être.* There is no clear line of authority within the group, nor any agenda. Any expectation on the part of any individual participant as to what the trainers are there for is quickly shattered by the experience of complete ambiguity.

As introduction, the group members are urged to concentrate on the group itself and its present problem of existence, rather than to deal with past experiences of individuals or to comment on extraneous events or issues. Many groups will contain members who have been in T-Groups before to make possible the effective introduction of the group to its task. The individual finds himself effectively thrown back on what can be called completely personal resources, as against intellectual or academic resources or reputation and categorical status. Each is there as a human person, with nothing but human personhood to offer or to lose. Members are expected and encouraged to express their true feelings as far as they can, including revealing to each other their true feelings about each other's comments, appearance, personality, and fears. Complete candor is essential, if an intellectual term can be applied to the phenomenon, and quickly becomes the norm since candor tends to breed itself.

External aspects of T-Groups vary, but matters of place and time are the only prearranged detail. Some are spread over many weeks at the rate of three or four hours a week, some are conducted intensively on a single weekend without respite. Avoidance of interruption is important if the group is to be genuinely microcosmic, and in weekend sessions the group will ideally carry on all functions together, including eating, sleeping, and relaxing. The groups are ideally coeducational. Adult criticism of this aspect of sensitivity training might well arise, but something far more important than sexual closeness is being sought here.

The intensity of the T-Group is obviously very high, and there are invariably some casualties in students who cannot stand the pressure of complete openness or complete directionlessness in group activity. The threads of the more delicate forms of sanity are stretched, wounds long covered up freshly exposed, and real psychological problems sometimes uncovered. Participants are cautioned, in the words of the Michigan literature, that the T-Group activity "is not intended to provide the kind of help that one would expect from psychotherapy or a counseling relationship," and more specifically, "a student who is currently in psychotherapy or thinking of entering it may wish to talk over with his therapist and trainers of Outreach T-Groups whether it would also be advisable to join a group at this time." The point is well taken, even in its somewhat euphemistic tone.

Because of the intensity of the experience, and in view of the goals of the T-Group as an example of sensitivity training, the role of the trainer is obviously of paramount importance. If he is too much given to intervention in the interests of his own view of how things should be going, he will destroy the opportunity for the microsociety to create itself out of its own resources. This may be merely a distraction, costing time, or it may be a permanent disorientation for the group. It would seem that the trainer is best cast when he plays a role similar to that of Bartleby in Melville's "Bartleby the Scrivener," and the feelings of the group resemble those of Bartleby's employer. The NTL literature speaks of trainers as "change agents . . . persons who can help others increase their skills in working relationships, problem solving and decision making." (Reading Book, p. 7) The best trainer is one who is capable himself, by training and comprehension of the theory of group relationships, of "refusing to carry out the traditional expectations of his role." (Reading Book, p. 7)

One T-Group exposure is not enough to accomplish the goals for any individual; it can do no more than introduce him to the problem and give him some confidence in the possibility of its solution. The student trainee, however, forms a deep loyalty to the experience, and for the most part to other members of his group. He regrets the necessary return to the workaday campus and looks forward to another opportunity for T-Group experience, particularly with the same group. The NTL literature points out that "the T-Group experience provides a safe 'arena' in which one's own feelings, and those of one's group fellows may be observed and *felt* and their consequences upon personal and group action observed." A considerable amount of trust is built up in those with whom one has shared this experience.

The controlled situation afforded by including sensitivity training in a psychology curriculum is far more acceptable than other means students have of getting into a sensitivity program. Many colleges have made funds available for student programing of T-Groups on their campuses, but most have not. Students are hard put to provide for themselves, organizationally speaking, the opportunity. I would observe that the character of T-Group sensitivity training is thus such as to be a disappointment in the search for salvation, for it seems it must be provided by some arm of the Establishment. It costs money and takes some organizational work. Trainers tend to be as amply booked into the future as lecturers. Moreover, although it seems to be tailor-made for the student search for salvation, I will show below that there are some aspects of its purpose that students should not accept.

Nonverbal Communication

The student society today is in many ways characterized by students trying to find out what their bodies are for. The drug experience, chemical in nature, destroyed for them the last vestiges of the mind-body dualism which the folk culture still entertained and introduced the idea of a holistic salvation as the most likely to be sought. One aspect of sensitivity training that commends itself most readily to students in this respect is nonverbal communication. There are many mechanical routines which release nonverbal communication, and the field for invention of others is entirely open. Here I mention only a few of the better known.

In one nonverbal communication exercise, for example, a group of eight or ten participants form a circle with one member in the middle. This member closes his eyes and starts to fall, but his body is caught by someone in the circle who then passes it on to someone else, the person either beside him or across the circle, or to whomever he chooses. With his feet relaxed but stationary, and making no effort to support himself, the subject will experience only the hands and their movements of those around him. Some will be tender, some rough, some panicky, some supremely confident. He will discover his own trust level and his own talent for wondering whether anyone in the group will betray (drop) him and who it will be. All participants in this exercise learn something about themselves that no amount of intellectual conversation can convey.

Another technique employed is one where the participants pair off, facing each other and pretending that they are images one of the other in a mirror. What one does, the other does. The subtle shifts of initiative for the action and the test of will either to control the action or to withstand the temptation to control it then constitute a kind of communication between the two participants.

Students are overwhelmed with words, in the books they read, in papers they write, and in classroom lectures and discussions. They are, moreover, subliminally convinced that the absence of words is the absence of communication. In this connection it is interesting to observe the difficulty that most teachers experience about allowing any silence during a class period, let alone any less than the required hours of class time in which to be talking or conducting discussion. If any really great ideas find expression within the structure of a lecture, it might be well to provide some time, other than as a histrionic gesture, for the idea to be absorbed and played with, rather than merely transferred to a notebook for later cogitation. That, of course, never takes place because the idea was not contained in the words, however accurately put down, but in the interrelationship between the persons in the class. Nonverbal communication has, therefore, for students at least the fascination of the bizarre. It has also constituted a saving release from the bondage to words which the college student's life seems to endure. It enhances his sensitivity to the ways in which he communicates with his peers and with his teachers and the ways in which they communicate with him beyond, underneath, and around the words that fly back and forth between them. It is revolutionary as well and has many implications for curriculum theory. But for the present it is so contradictory to the general pattern of college life that it seems saving. It is no wonder that students avidly seek this kind of activity. It is too seldom noticed that the music of today and the great enthusiasm for films on the campus are further evidence of the importance assigned to nonverbal communication.

THE PROMISE OF SALVATION

The ideals of an ample sensitivity seem naïve to any adult who has long since made his peace with gaps in his own and others' credibility. It is no more than a garden-variety insight into oneself to realize the problem of seeing "ourselves as others see us." The tremendous popularity of Eric Berne's *Games People Play* has been due more to its complete familiarity than to its educative importance. The Freudian axiom of the power of the latent, hidden content of any behavior over the manifest, overt intention of it is part of folk wisdom by now, and the religious insight that a man's actions are to be judged in the light of his intentions is very old. But the students' search for salvation is at every point the desire to bring together the many and diverse worlds in which they find themselves, and the mild disjuncture of will and woe in the behavior of those around them, and of themselves, is of serious concern. Only the cynic can argue that our universal insights into our emotional ineptitude at being what we intend to be should simply be accepted.

Students are fascinated with sensitivity training because of the lure of becoming better persons as a result of participation in it. That is the form of salvation it offers. But the question it immediately raises is: "What good is it to be a better person if no clearer knowledge of what you are better for is given?" The hidden difficulty in sensitivity training is its assumption that sensitivity is a sufficiently radical virtue that no other purpose in or definition of better personhood is needed.

Students generally are unaware that the techniques so effective in releasing them from the conflict between their defenses and their talents are equally effective in unlocking any particular talents for whatever purpose they may be used. The occupational fields to which human-resources experimentation has been applied include not only the world of education but also industrial management, government, community organizations, and a variety of particular major industries that have had the sense to see its value. In a discussion of the three rough categorizations of leadership, the Tough Battler, the Friendly Helper, and the Objective Thinker, all of whom impede smooth functioning of group process by their personality formations and their conflict with each other, the NTL literature speaks of how each can be made more effective as "manager, father, neighbor, person." (Reading Book, p. 18)

The real purpose of sensitivity training seems to be simply to make groups function better, no matter what groups they are or what their purpose for coming together is. Presumably sensitivity training is valuable to industrial corporations because it makes for smoother teamwork in the organization and fewer abrasions on the individual in group work. The final product in the student's world is that it will make him a better student! Indeed his life will be more satisfying if that eventuality were attained and if along the way his teachers were to become better teachers, but I think it would not then be the salvific blessing he now sees it to be at a time when the contrasts between the sensitized and the insensitive are so vivid. The purpose of his education and the purpose of his later life would remain untouched. The final goal of sensitivity training would be our present society doing what it is already doing only more efficiently and with greater cooperation among all its elements. While that is obviously a necessity it is very different from the questions students are raising about the goals and direction of that society functioning as zigzaggedly as it now does.

THE PROMISE EVALUATED

Sensitivity training has a fascination arising from the hope of universality, but the success of sensitizing an entire population would create a situation no different from the present. The University of Michigan psychology course literature seems to realize this without realizing its macabre implications when it says that the result of successful T-Group work is "an upward spiral of openness leading to warmth and mutual concern and these lead to more openness." The real tragedy in American society, or in any group within it, is that sensitivity training and the sensitizing of individuals are necessary. I am not for a moment arguing that it is not, only that it is not a final answer to questions students are raising. It is, like drugs, therapeutically necessary, and it is sad that there are so many college students who need this therapy, just as it is mandatory that they have it soon. The secret of it, they should easily learn, is that many can do it themselves. Then it will take on a different character. Otherwise they may be participating in a movement which might just as well be occupied in making the delicate human cogs in the Pentagon function so amiably with one another that we can engineer napalm attacks on any trouble spot on the globe at an efficient moment's notice. What students seek in the T-Group is salvation. What they get is the hidden agenda of Establishmentarianism. The NTL literature argues that if people can be in on the experience of the creation of a segment of society "they would come to understand on cognitive, feeling and operational levels, the great need for both order and change, and the delicate relationship and balance that must lie between them." They would be effectively talked out of facing down the American educational institution on the question of its true purpose, and this may be the only saving thing they have to offer.

Until the *parousia,* when all are sensitized, there are limitations on the value of this movement for individual students. There is the necessity of making use of their sensitivity in application of their talents to the creation of beauty, truth, and goodness in the world. The artist or poet could be effectively sidetracked from the act of creation if he sees his problem in the truncated personal milieu of the group expert. There needs to be time in a student's life for work, and the effectiveness of sensitivity training should be to show him where the line has to be drawn to discover what his true work is. It has to include some utter privacy. It has to include some silence—an older form of nonverbal communication. It has to include his successful relationship with the things of the world, not just the people. If hallucinogenic drugs limit the perspective of the individual to himself and the chemical reactions of his own body, sensitivity training tends to limit the perspective of the individual to himself in his capacity for interpersonal relations. To overstate it, a sensitivity aficionado should read in Buber's *I and Thou* about the possibility of relationship with a tree or a cat. Our society is in part in its present danger because it has proceeded on the basis that people are the only problem, rather than seeing that people are only partly the problem because we are unrelated to things. Salvation will be a way to avoid responsibility for destroying the material of this world just as surely as it will be a way to avoid undue hurt of another person.

But even on the interpersonal level, the insensitivity of the rest of us being what it is, the sensitized individual is encouraged to seek salvation in another world-within-the-world of his own artificial construction. The task is not to see what is involved in creating a social organization, but to see what happens when the world we already have threatens to destroy itself (an idea with which it is apparently willing to live), what happens when students discover that they can *remake* the world they live in and set out to try.

Again it is on the basis of the search for salvation that the enthusiasm for and interest in sensitivity training has hit the campus. The futility of the means in this case is again no effective commentary on the seriousness of the search. American society, by promoting defensiveness, has required its young to waste a lot of time and energy in recovering sensitiveness. While many students will feel that sensitivity training *is* salvation and will be lost to the task of remaking their world because it is a side track, many others will simply be more determined in their search as a result of seeing the shallowness of what sensitivity training offers. Sensitive they must be, but more than sensitivity is needed to support the continuing search for salvation. Not least is the need to discipline sensitivity, as artist and poet do, so that it is brought to burning focus on those issues that impede salvation. Some students attempt to find such discipline in religion.

4

SEARCHING AMONG THE RELIGIONS

For I am the sacrifice and the offering, the sacred
    gift and the sacred plant. I am the holy words,
    the holy food, the holy fire, and the offering that
    is made in the fire.
I am the Father of this universe, and even the Source
    of the Father. I am the Mother of this universe, and
    the Creator of all. I am the Highest to be known,
    the Path of purification, the holy OM, the Three Vedas.

—Bhagavad Gita 9, 16–17

Although the salvation that the church attempts to offer is
rejected by college students, the search for salvation does
take place in religious exploration. When what students
are doing takes them into religious activity, it is clearer
that the search for salvation is the proper model for understanding their life. It is to the various forms of this that we
now turn; but first it is necessary to be more specific about
the rejection of the family church in the search for salvation. And what is said about the church goes for the
family synagogue as well, which is formally indistinguishable from its Christian neighbors.

THE STUDENTS' PRECOLLEGE RELIGIOUS EXPERIENCE

What I have called the psychological and sociological discoveries of students amount to a suspicion that the church

has for some time been defining its mission in America in purely functional terms, that it has capitalized on the psychological and sociological lore of this century as an excuse for its being. Thus it serves a real purpose for anyone whose self-description and whose view of society is also dependent on this lore, which is the case for most of the adult world. The church, then, offers itself to the individual in a kind of sheltering and solacing way as an escape from the threatening ambiguity of the rest of one's life. In the fashion of a loan company offering to consolidate debts by the device of an umbrella loan, the church trades the many enervating illusions of the individual for its own grand illusion of a programed salvation in creed, sermon, and ecclesiastical structure, just as Freud said it could. And socially, the church has accepted its role of being the confirming and cohesive agent for a fragmented and pluralistic culture. Will Herberg's analysis of the Americanization of the immigrant religious traditions in *Protestant-Catholic-Jew* is rather old now, but it still explains how most adults, the parents of college students *par excellence,* see the role and function of the church in America.

In both circumstances, the church is essentially dishonest and shows itself to be concerned pre-eminently with its own relevance to the surrounding society. (In a later chapter we shall examine the student shibboleth of "relevance"— much criticized by their elders—but the students' criticism of their family churches comes down to this: it has been too relevant to American life.) Students sense the essential lack of seriousness in the churches' preoccupation with survival and sniff out the motive of self-preservation in every activity to which they have been exposed. As in school, they have not been treated as persons, but as contributors to the life of an institution. Their "youth group" (if they got that far before dropping out of church) was more important than any of its members were. After all, the youth are the future leaders of the church, it was always said, as if some ulterior justification were necessary.

If they sense a lack of seriousness in the life of the church, there is plain doubtfulness about what the church is serious about. This is not merely a matter of taking the easy road of shouting hypocrisy to an ecclesiastical father. It is the pressure of genuine intellectual doubt as much as anything else. For what the churches do take seriously tends to be a claim to the utter reasonableness of the Christian faith (or in the synagogues, of the Jewish life). The pulpits of America are deftly apologetic and have related church doctrine to each intellectual phenomenon of our experience, precisely in order to show that the faith is not ill at ease with any of man's worlds. But the lady protests too much, and the church is assumed by students to be very ill at ease indeed with questions and doubts.

Add to this the observation that all religious experience in the life of American churches, almost without exception, is secondhand. A student has to go far back into early adolescence to remember anything like a religious experience. He is easily the boy in James Agee's *The Morning Watch,* but the childhood numinous moment has not reappeared as he has matured. Nor, and this is more significant, has anyone around him expected it to reappear or encouraged him to expect it to do so. His minister, likely as not, would have been embarrassed to discuss it with him. His parents would have thought it a regression to childhood. And neither minister nor parent would have given any evidence of any authentic religious experience of his own. For decades now, applications to seminaries have asked prospective students to describe the nature of their call to the ministry. For decades, applicants have hastened to insist that they have "seen no visions, heard no voices," but have gradually and naturally gravitated to this vo-

cation "to help people." So far as I know, the theological
schools have blessed and accepted this pattern, and have
been suspicious of any exceptions to it, so that today's college student has been exposed to religious traditions without any direct, personal, experiential meaning in them for
him apart from what he can intellectually impose on
them. A religious person today is almost required to be a
gifted historian and "live himself back into" another day to
find out what religion is about. If they read it, students
would delight in Kierkegaard's *Attack Upon Christendom,*
except that they could write it themselves. Their view of
what their family religion has given them is that it tells
them about profound experiences other (and past) people
have had of religious truths. No way of having it themselves is ever suggested.

The students will also point out the sensory inadequacy
of religious activity. This tends to be true even when they
come out of sacramental religious traditions where the body
and blood of Christ is eaten and drunk in worship. Again,
the difficulty is that the churches, even the Catholic Church
of both pre- and post-Vatican Council II, have seemed
embarrassed about the primitive simplicity of this rite and
have intellectualized it as a doctrinal truth to be mentally
ingested rather than viscerally realized. In effect, this is a
rejection of religion by the church, and the rejection of the
church in the name of religion is justified.

It is a remarkable fact that relationship with college
chaplains is an exception to the rejection of the church. It
would be more accurate to say that it is a form of that
rejection, especially where it is clear, as it often is, that the
chaplain rejects the same church the students do (which
is often the reason he is a college chaplain). Partly because
he is the only person on the campus free from Establishment tensions to a sufficient extent to be interested and
available on a genuinely personal basis, and in that role he

drifts into competencies such as draft counseling (particularly of conscientious objectors), and partly because (as Myron Bloy has pointed out) he is marginal to the life of the institution and of society and is thus recognizable as an outsider with some apparent sympathy for the outsider-hood of the student, the chaplain is likely to find himself today incredibly busy and well occupied with students.

Paul Goodman surprised both his friends and his critics by observing this in the *New Republic* (January 7, 1967) and by noting that the church (as he saw it on college campuses) "so long a pillar of orthodox society, has begun to recall, dimly, that it has something to do with humanity, with divinity." His remarks confirm the point being made that religious exploration is the form which rejection of the church sometimes takes, and that the chaplain recognizes the validity and importance of this search: "In my observation it is an error to say that the present-day young are not interested in religion in a metaphysical sense. . . . They counter the discontents of civilization with a hankering for primitive experience, the complicated socialization with a desperate effect for personal communion, the complicated technology with experimental sacraments to produce instant salvation, the computer rationalism with a willingness to go crazy—temporarily. . . . Chaplains who say that students are interested in action but not in religion should ponder the implications of the student word 'commitment.' "

The pressure from the family church is, in my opinion, so heavy and so great an impediment to religious communication, that experiments with worship must begin right from scratch or be doomed to oblivion. No amount of *liturgical* experimentation seems possible to counteract the mindset which church involves. On a typical church-related college campus with an imposing chapel in the middle of everything, I have discovered that the building itself alone escapes this stricture. The building is widely used—by individuals and small knots of students in the middle of the night, talking, thinking together, "relating." Accordingly, I have determined that the building itself can take care of any ecclesiastical obligations I have, leaving us free to get on with the business of the search for salvation in religion. One result of this has been a corporate use of the building, late at night, for occasions that have no structure, no liturgy, no plan, and little similarity from one time to another. Students come. But they don't think of it as "going to church." There is nothing particularly flashy about what goes on on these occasions, but the lack of seriousness has at least been overcome. There is an area of human experience, as Michael Novak has argued, where belief and unbelief come to the same thing, can exist side by side, and are not committed to destroying each other. If this were possible in churches, they might be much less affluent, but much more religious.

The themes that we noted as appearing in the hallucinogenic drug experience, and in the activities of sensitivity training, insofar as these are seen on the religious model we are using, include a high emphasis on the importance of feeling, a discovery of the value of sensory openness, and a regard for whatever conduces to unifying an individual's experience, either in himself or with others. These are nothing if not religious themes and characterize the students' search for salvation in religious exploration as much as in any other student activity. It is demanded of that which claims to be religious that it do something to oneself, rather than just lie there as a museum piece or be available only to the intellect. Whatever the overt activity of recognizable churches will be in the future, there will have to be attention to these themes, not because they are needs to be met or fads to be followed, but because in uncovering these themes in their search, students have exposed the genteel glossing over of them by church life. To contrast the formality of the average church service (or the contrived carefulness of its mod successor, the folk masses and happenings) with what students are looking for is like comparing the society page of a newspaper with the real lives of its readers. Moreover, the juridical insistence of the church on a particular morality that is closely identified with the American national spirit compares badly with the kind of motivation that sends a college student into VISTA, community organizing, or to work in an institution for retarded children. They are simply different worlds, and the morality that students hear from their churches and synagogues is a morality that for long lay undisturbed by racism and war.

Because of his regard for unifying experience, the student is predictably impatient with the pluralistic god of American religion, so much so that he is in danger of a serious breach of tolerance. What the fine line is between tolerance and mere pluralism, no one yet seems to know, but the fads about "doing your own thing," and this or that being, or not being, my "bag," represent the paradox that is logically necessary in a world viewed pluralistically. The student, in fact, sees unity in religious consciousness more readily than the most tolerant of ecumenists, and to him the "ecumenical movement" is simply irrelevant. It tends now to be an assumption rather than a goal. Denominational consciousness is virtually completely gone from them, and they perform the consummate ecumenical act of rejecting all churches without bias or favoritism.

His "Academic" Study of Religion

The academic study of religion provides one opportunity for religious exploration which students have taken up with considerable enthusiasm. The past decade has seen a re-markable increase in the number and quality of course of-ferings in religion in colleges, both public and private. No longer do they tend to be the "gut" Bible courses taught by retired missionaries in church colleges. The undergradu-ate study of religion has now become a field of immense variety and professional self-consciousness. Annual meet-ings of the American Academy of Religion and the Society for the Scientific Study of Religion are well attended and testify that religion is finally taking its place alongside other academic disciplines with complete respectability. Teachers in the field guard jealously the reputation of their work to assure its integrity in the curriculum and boast, with some justification, that relatively few of their majors are bound for the ministry. Some have begun to be concerned that the academic teaching of religion is becoming the new re-ligious establishment. Students in many institutions may now take courses in Buddhism or Islam, in the Johannine writings of the New Testament or in the mythology of Plato, in the Dead Sea Scrolls or in Primitive Religion. I have known students in recent years who, as undergradu-ates, have done serious independent research into such disparate areas as the development of the concept of tra-dition in the early church fathers and the visionary apoca-lypticism of William Blake.

Paradoxically, while the faculty have made available a rich buffet of religious studies by increasing the academic seriousness of the field, religion is the one area to which students gravitate precisely because it is something they can study that is not "academic." ("Academic," always with the implied pejorative "mere," is a Bad Word in colleges, just as it is elsewhere in society. To faculty, "academic integrity" is an O.K. term, although to students it remains a mystery.) Invariably students will give as a reason for wanting to take a course in religion a hope that they can study something important to themselves, that it will give them a chance to find out who they are, that it will aid them personally. To become a religion major is tantamount to dropping out, motivationally. The impasse thus incurred between teachers and students of religion is not widely noticed as yet, and in fact the students solve it by taking what they want from religion courses and letting the faculty have their way for the rest of it, usually with good grace. Since education proceeds along the two tracks of which we have taken notice, there is an amiable generosity in students to recognize that the faculty get more out of what they are doing than their students do. Religion courses differ only in that students come into them with existential questions, seeking answers to life's problems. It is a search for salvation.

WHAT THIS STUDY PROVIDES

What academic study of religion provides and what the churches lack is precisely that seriousness of purpose in the approach to and discussion of religion which marks it as saving. A college religion course may be the first time a student has ever really been interested in theology. His mind is "blown" by Tillich on ultimate concern, Buber's concept of I-Thou, and Rudolf Otto's insistence on the indispensability of religious experience and his moving evocation of it in *The Idea of the Holy*. He is not likely to be quite so impressed with *The Secular City* or with radical theology, but he will bring to these a serious criticism based on his intuitions about what deserves to be called religious. The irony is that at the same time professional theologians were expressing themselves in terms of the concept of secularity, students were becoming more interested in the transcendent and the sacred. When students discovered that radical theology is essentially apolitical, they found it to that extent something less than radical, proving, in my view, that rejection of the family church is not the only motive in the religious search. By contrast most "political theology" tends to be ecclesiastically conservative. Students accept its politics but not its theology. Martin Luther King, Jr., in most students' estimation, heard a drummer far different from that apparent in his religious tradition. The task of bringing together a genuinely radical theology with the radical political outlook of college students has yet to be accomplished, although writings are beginning to appear in this area.

When students are not offered, or are not able to take advantage of, religious exploration in academic study of religion, they search it out for themselves, particularly in study and work with Eastern religions. In our college we stocked *The Teachings of the Compassionate Buddha* in the bookshop as required reading for one particular course but had to reorder a second and again a third time before the students enrolled in the course could all obtain copies. For before they could pick up their copies, others, not in the course, bought them out from under them. One had the vision of a sizable segment of the campus turned on to the Buddhist sermons, and, to the horror of some faculty, without academic supervision! Virtually anything in the field of Eastern religions will be bought and read by students in this form of private search.

STUDENT INTEREST IN EASTERN RELIGIONS

Eastern religions, as a subject within religious studies, is itself an enormous and varied field. No one can master it easily or quickly, if ever. There is justification for observing that the students' interest in this case is simply interest in the arcane and the bizarre. To be sure, there is a popular side to this form of the search for salvation, nowhere better evidenced than in the continuing popularity of *The Prophet,* by Kahlil Gibran, or in the brief celebrity of the Maharishi Mahesh Yogi. A parent of a student of mine, upset about her son's having left college rather suddenly and having disappeared westward, announced to me that they had been able to handle the drug phase without too much difficulty, but did I not think he might be going off the deep end with all this meditation business? This student had with complete artlessness passed on to me his dogeared Xerox copy of the instruction in transcendental meditation which he had mastered before going off to seek his fortune, and peace. To him and others, meditation took them beyond drugs, but it failed to prepare them for its own complex implications.

If it is true that a lot that could not be serious is taken up by students under the "Eastern religions" umbrella, it is also the case that the popular literature encountered in this search contains some gems. Hermann Hesse's *Siddharta* is a case in point, a Western book about the Buddha which has given many students more sense than they had any right to hope for. And at the least, study of texts like the *Bhagavad Gita* confirms the sense of distance (or perhaps loss?) which the cultural heritage imposes on them in depriving them of a thing of real power and beauty.

Generalizations about Eastern religions are "unacademic," but it is possible to set down what it is that students find useful and stimulating in their search. Discovering what they gained from the literature and lore of those religious traditions foreign to their backgrounds confirms that they are not merely in generational revolt but genuinely in search for something.

Explanatory confidence. Explanation of the mysteries of human existence and of the way the world works as seen from a religious vantage point has long since been left behind in Western religion. The eighteenth century was a crisis in explanation for the Jewish-Christian world-view, for it was then that explanation as a possibility began to be invested in empirical observation. The reductionism of this shift in Western intellectual life has been compensated by a vast increase in the amount of scientific explanation possible, but it is still remarkable that so many of the questions that plagued the prescientific world plague us still, questions of meaning, evil, death, guilt, and purpose. Since the religious thought of Western Christendom comes to the student filtered through the cautious and confining milieu of scientific agnosticism, it comes as a relief to encounter in writings from the East an explanatory confidence about the basic questions of human existence. The cosmology of transcendental meditation may be false, but at least it is not cautious or provisional. We have still to respond intellectually to William James's observation that our culture is terrified of metaphysical error. We have only solved it by deciding that the metaphysical, since beyond proof, is unimportant. Eastern religious texts, whether Buddhist, Hindu, or Confucianist, tend to redress this caution, urging the devout to see the world around him in a certain way with assurance and conclusiveness.

Spiritual direction. Because college students have difficulty getting into the classics of Christian or Jewish spirituality, their response to Eastern religion is often a response to the directness of specifically religious language in religious texts. Too much of American religion hesitates on the brink of real spiritual guidance, in exercises by which the individual might train himself in religious consciousness, for fear that it will not be able to answer the cultural, scientific "why" that lurks behind every possibility in Western life. The individual first becoming acquainted with Eastern religious traditions is surprised at the directness with which he is told to do this or that piece of business as a religious exercise, without any nondirective qualification about it. The last six chapters of the Gita are full of such commands, to give only one example.

Sensory relevance. Although it is but an aspect of spiritual direction, the religious importance of sensory experience strikes the student of Eastern religions as providing something sadly missing from his religious background. He is told to cultivate his seeing, his hearing, his touch, his smell in order to bring them under mastery and use them in the service of the spirit. The implicit dualism of Western religion, wherein the object is to escape the body, is transcended in a generally more humane confidence that in this life is the beginning of any other life. Diet, posture, breathing, and feeling are made use of in religious exercises. For most students, it has been a long time since they heard a sermon in the family church speaking so directly to their real lives.

These constitute, admittedly, a kind of *escape* from the strictures of Western religion in its intellectualized and moralized presentation of itself to its devotees. But religion, as a cooperating institution in Western society, has produced a world in which there is a great deal to escape from. Moreover, the effect of this tends not to be mere escape for those who maintain seriousness about it, but rather an effective reorientation of their view of life which confirms their alienation from much of American society and freshly commits them to its change. When Allen Ginsberg led a crowd of college students in a mantra in Lincoln Park in

Chicago, 1968, it had the makings of a genuine religious celebration. It provided a strength in confrontation with the Establishment many of them might not have had otherwise. Also, since college students are and will remain Westerners, the real importance of the search for salvation in Eastern religions will be to steadily increase the pressure against the assumptions of Western religion, causing it to reform itself in the light of these discoveries. A great deal in the Western tradition will be rediscovered; thus the re-introduction into church life of a great deal that has embarrassed the modern church may come about in the relatively near future.

The late Thomas Merton has written effectively on this point in *Mystics and Zen Masters*. He observed that the Ecumenical Movement has lamentably ignored the ecumenism of spirituality in its doctrinal work. Noting that dialogue with Eastern contemplatives found him feeling more in common with them than with most of his fellow Catholics, Merton suggests an interpenetration of Eastern and Western mysticism as the new (and real) ecumenism to which religion is called. The explorations of the college students both buttress this suggestion and provide the hope that it may be implemented.

OBSERVATIONS ON A CASE IN POINT

We can perhaps best illustrate what might emerge by reference to a concrete case. Two students who were open to Eastern religious experience yet conscious of their presence in Western culture came to the writer to be married, but with extensive plans of their own for the wedding. My critics dubbed it a "hippie wedding," but I hope to show that it evoked a seriousness not often present in the "church wedding."

First, in planning the wedding, the couple wanted to "do it themselves," in order to make it as meaningful as possible in communicating to them and their friends the emotional depth of the occasion. This sort of thing is usually taken care of by the florist and caterer and by the charged mothering atmosphere that wants everything "to go right." This couple wanted everything to *be* right, a perfectionist hope, but a refreshing change. Conversation established my views on what parts of the marriage service seemed to me essential in substance: some declaration of purpose, exchange of vows and ring(s), proclamation of marriage and blessing. The form of marriage service in the Episcopal Book of Common Prayer is euphemistic and florid, imposing on the marriage situation a creditable doctrine of marriage but imposing a lot else besides. Revision of the language was a first necessity. Here is a sample, the declaration of purpose:

We are here to join this man and this woman in marriage. Marriage is the act whereby these persons will give themselves to each other for the rest of their lives, in the name of love and so that they might seek to grow together in love. In this service we try to give expression to this love and to symbolize in various ways the total exchange which a true marriage requires, and have added to the usual service elements which elaborate the exchange and identify it as the profound recognition of our nature which we believe it to be.

Jesus told some of his critics once: Have you read that he which made them in the beginning made them male and female, and said, for this cause a man shall leave father and mother, and shall be joined to his wife, and they shall be one flesh? Then they are no longer two, but one flesh. What God has joined together, man must not separate.

To be joined together in this way, these two people have now come. If anyone can show cause why they may not lawfully be joined together, let him now speak or else afterward keep silence.

Similarly, passages like the ring exchange were simplified to: "With this ring I marry you, in the name of God. Amen."

Such revisions were only a first step. The couple spent a good deal of time planning the other elements which would "elaborate the exchange" and give expression to what they felt for each other. Music was provided by a stereo record player, the prelude being one of the love *ragas* played by Ravi Shankar, the postlude a Vivaldi flute concerto. To all the student participants this was a natural pair of choices; the only thing remarkable was their hearing them in a church! Following the prelude and before the entrance of the bride and groom, the best man came forward (attired in Levis and a corduroy jacket) and read from the everpresent Kahlil Gibran, a choice I would have vetoed had I approached the service in a different spirit. Though more schmaltz than substance, its advice is not too unsound:

> Love one another, but make not a bond of love;
> Let it rather be a moving sea between the
>   shores of your souls.
> Fill each other's cup but drink not from one cup.
> Give one another of your bread but eat not from
>   the same loaf.
> Sing and dance together and be joyous, but
>   let each one of you be alone,
> Even as the strings of a lute are alone though
>   they quiver with the same music . . .
>
> Stand together yet not too near together:
> For the pillars of the temple stand apart,
> And the oak trees and the cypress grow not
>   in each other's shadow.*

* From Kahlil Gibran, *The Prophet* (New York: Alfred A. Knopf, 1923), pp. 15–16. Used with permission.

Following the exchange of rings, an oracle was read from the *I Ching*. The oracle had been cast the morning of the wedding, and served as a kind of topical homily, its content general enough to be mildly inspirational to a Western religious mind, its tone just solemn enough not to invade the celebrative mood and manner of the participants. The *I Ching,* one of the Four Books of Confucianism, is a book of divination into which was distilled the prophetic wisdom by which the Chou dynasty justified itself in ancient China. The fatalism of the oracles should be noted, but even this contrasts freshly with the homely but absurd wisdom that is given voice at most conventional weddings. The best man read the oracle. Then "love beads" were exchanged with the words:

> Groom: "I am the sky, you are the earth. Come,
>   let us marry."
> Bride: "I am the earth, you are the sky. Come,
>   let us marry."

As their own choice, the bride and groom then read antiphonally to each other the Thirty-third Psalm (vv. 3–5):

> Sing unto the Lord a new song; sing praises
>   lustily unto him with a good courage.
> For the word of the Lord is true; and all his
>   works are faithful.
> He loveth righteousness and judgment; the
>   earth is full of the goodness of the Lord.

Such a service as this has the danger of being, in Merton's words, a "loose and irresponsible syncretism" but, unless imitated beyond its newness and individuality, has the advantage of freshness and of having engaged the participants fairly thoroughly in research into their religious views as a preparation for the occasion.

The contrast with the usual wedding verges on unkindness. Couples being married seldom bring any real concern to what is said or how it is done at all, so long as it is done with propriety and so long as relatives and friends recognize the little rituals of etiquette which have effectively ruined marriage traditions in American churches. Despite a firm conviction in Catholic religious traditions that the ministers in the sacrament of matrimony are the bride and groom, that they marry each other, usually it is a matter of being married by a minister who "performs the service." Careful preparation for marriage may overcome some of this insouciance about its religious content, but preparation *of* the service itself *by* the bride and groom to give expression to their real religious views is a lesson altogether untried. In this case it was not only a clear example of the search for salvation, a station on the way to religious seriousness, but also a very moving and happy occasion.

Not everyone would be happy about such a venture, and not everyone in this case was. The dress of all participants was the thing singled out by relatives who thought it execrable. But it was comfortable, and it was not a costume ball. Students would do well to see the occasions of their marriage and other celebrations as possible moments when their search for salvation can make decisive steps of progress, and to demand a voice in their planning.

The search for salvation in religion, then, runs from rejection of family church tradition, through academic and extracurricular study of religion, into Eastern religious attractions, and on to inventiveness in the construction of ceremonies for its observance. It is characterized by the instinct for unity, the emphasis upon experiencing and the necessity to do, not just to think, in the religious sphere. In drugs, sensitivity experience, and religious exploration the religious model allows us to observe the search for salvation in experience entered upon by the individual for his *own* salvation. It is, to a certain extent, the limitation of individual salvation that is proclaimed by the equally important external, social, and moral demands of college students for salvation for *others*, for the destruction of the impediments to salvation which society has allowed to grow to such size and complexity, specifically war, racism, and poverty. The search for salvation in religion continues while the search for salvation of others in activism, relevance, and revolution proceeds.

5

SAVING ACTIVISM

. . . never send to know for whom
the bell tolls; it tolls for thee.

—John Donne

When they knock over there, fella,
They're knockin' for you.

—Phil Ochs

Student activism has been with us long enough, and has a
history sufficiently diverse, to warrant our inspecting it in
the terms of the model we have been using—namely, the
search for salvation. One would indeed hope that this history will provide both the foundation for future activities
and the promise of a more just social structure. Let my
mention of this hope, however, serve as a serious caveat to
my readers *and* to sensitive students because it informs in
many ways the perspective from which this chapter is
written. The character and quality of this hope were precisely delineated by Tom Kahn in 1966 when he wrote the
following in *Commentary* (July, 1966): "There are those,
among whom I include myself, who criticize out of a hope
growing nearly desperate that this outburst of radical dis-
content will stick, that it will sink deep roots, that it will

energize a new political movement, and transform national institutions—in short, that its legacy to the next generation will be a new beginning, not that tiresome mixture of cynicism and nostalgia that grows out of defeat and hangs over us (of the old Left) still." And to Kahn's statement I would add that the *hope* which he expressed has been amply confirmed since his statement of it, while simultaneously, the *desperation* born of reaction and the repression of student activist energies has also grown apace. Activism, as I see it, faces the impossible assignment of walking on eggs: of not losing its inventive and enthusiastic spirit while for some time to come failing in most of its goals.

THE NEW ELEMENT IN SALVATION

Activism, basically, is the implementation of the rhetoric of idealism through behavior calculated to expose the complacency of those agents of oppression who knowingly or unknowingly perpetuate injustice and inhumanity. It is grounded on the perception that rhetoric in itself is merely rhetoric, and unproductive of reform. It becomes the external, physical manifestation of alienation, which may either confirm or deflate the realism of alienation by either effectively proving the objective basis for alienation or by exposing it as the fantasy of a few or of a type. It is the attempt to prove, then, that injustice is remediable within one's own society, a process which involves the hazard of discovering that injustice is only imagined.

Activism has succeeded in the past decade in exposing real diseases in our social body. Its present task is to maintain this exposure effectively enough to assure some research into the cure, and at the same time to plot any further necessary course of action. Activism can be a flash in the pan, explicable in terms of social psychology, or it can be a genuine turning point in the vocation of the young within society. Because it is, by definition, external and public, there will always be the temptation to define it out of existence rather than to help it find energy for new directions. It is because of hope "growing nearly desperate" that such temptations will be resisted here. If to students my comments and observations seem overly critical, I trust that they will also realize that what I say is in the interest of more, not less, activism. If, on the other hand, what I say seems irresponsible to my peers and elders, then so be it; I shall have succeeded in my purpose of putting into words the frightening yet saving process of activism.

To begin to understand activism as a saving force, one's perspective moves from the inward-looking salvation of the individual to salvation of another dimension. One can justifiably categorize activism as salvational because activist projects have had demonstrably positive and reforming results both in eliminating impediments to salvation and in effecting change. What I am concerned to make clear, however, is that our chief justification in categorizing activism as saving lies in the fact that in activism salvation is sought on a new and exceedingly important level, namely, that of salvation for others. Attendant upon this goal, as a corollary, is the further insight—and to me the most compelling evidence of its having reached a new level—that is, an awareness that salvation for oneself is not in the final analysis possible apart from salvation for others. This is an essentially altruistic insight whenever it appears, although "altruism" seems altogether too bland a word for characterizing it adequately. To students this is the essential unitive insight that they find missing in our social organization and social institutions. Most important and significant, however, is the fact that within this insight is the seed of genuine social renewal. When contrasted with the celebrated noninvolvement of earlier generations of college students in America, the current activism represents nothing less than a rediscovery of the environment, of the world around them, and of the plight of others. It is the discovery that the ominous knock on the door, which can now be heard almost everywhere in the world, is one that says, "They're knockin' for you." Thus activism begins in, and continues to confirm, the identity which the activist feels with all who are objects of social or political malevolence.

It has frequently been observed that student opposition to the Vietnam War is naïve and misguided when it points to the barbarous techniques of warfare that have been exposed by the nightly newscasts. War has always been hell, it is argued, and this one cannot be expected to be different. Yet there is an important sense in which it is different because of the character and extent of our exposure to it. The evil of evil, after all, is clear not only to those who have to endure it but to those who, through proximity and a sense of responsibility, empathize with and have compassion for the sufferers. It is the necessity that the media produce in the viewer of participating in evil that creates the "problem of evil," that gives focus to the evil of evil. The proximity to war-born suffering, which all Americans now know, is greater, more extensive than ever in our history, and appears particularly so to a generation reared in a context where reality is at least partly gauged by television programing so that their very closeness to a scene easily becomes participation. Moreover their sense of responsibility increases as their sense of participation intensifies. Thus the war in Vietnam has been a hell of a different war than ever before. Whatever the outcome in social reform, everybody now participates in war. That some, and particularly the idealistic young, should find themselves empathizing with its victims cannot be surprising.

The identity with the oppressed which activism presupposes is remarkable in its extension. It is the search for the human, not merely for the American or for one's own particular kind or class of American, which is at issue. It is not, in the usual sense of the term, un-American thereby, for the kind of patriotism involved is a genuine love of place directed at America and simultaneously a rejection of the superficialities of patriotism, which pass for love of country in adult society. It is the kind of love of country which is hurt to see America despised and feared. It is the kind of love of country which senses a suicidal course in anti-Communism as well as in the plundering of America's beauty. It recognizes that to be an American is to be able to do anything in this world but only at the expense of many people within America and many more outside it whose aspirations (or even survival) are denied when the issue is to protect American interests. A rich idealism emanates from the American history our children have been taught, and one rather crude way of putting what it does to and for them is to say that they don't see why everybody cannot have the benefits we enjoy in this society. The effect of this query is to turn these benefits sour.

Activism is then required to express the truth of this evaluation and to challenge our affluence on the basis of our identification with others, in and out of American life, whose limited and shabby participation in the richness of human life is in itself a challenge to our complacent enjoyment of affluence. For the individual seeking various means of salvation, no society has ever provided more easy ways out. It is also possible that no society has ever programed itself against real human unity more effectively than ours. To expose the essential disunity of our social life, then, is one of the purposes of any activist project.

THE LESSONS OF STUDENT ACTIVIST EXPERIENCE

Nowhere is such a view of activism more defensible than in the successive waves of activism on campuses directed at racism and at the war in Vietnam. Student activists did not invent the civil rights movement, of course, but early in the 60's, students discovered it under the pressure of the insight that there is no salvation for the individual without the salvation of others. In this context this realization took the form that there is no pleasure in maturing into full participation in American society when that participation was systematically denied to blacks. The Student Nonviolent Coordinating Committee used thousands of student volunteers to assist in voter registration in the South, and until the beginnings of the Black Power era in 1966, the civil rights movement was as much the students' cause as anyone's. During the same period another aspect of civil rights arose in the plight of Appalachia, and one of the early activities of the Students for a Democratic Society in the Fall of 1962 was to attempt to give assistance to the miners' movement in Eastern Kentucky. It was perhaps naïve of student activists to expect that racial unity was possible in American life, and the failure of both the civil rights movement as such and of student participation in civil rights activity is instructive in demonstrating some of the difficulties in keeping activism saving.

The Kerner Commission report was the final stage in a massive revelatory experience in American life, not unlike, in form, the revelatory experiences of biblical times in which truth manifested itself in historical events characterizing and forming a society. The events which occurred in American life beginning with the rebellion in Watts were clear enough, but events are mere items in a chronicle until they are trenchantly interpreted in a manner sufficient to show their effect and their import. The truth bursting through the events was that a deeper division cut through American life than many whites would admit, a division that could not be healed by acts of assistance and good will. The only way in which this truth as the real interpretation of the meaning of the rebellion-events could be expressed clearly and accurately was in the uncompromising proposition that our society is racist. Although the proposition has yet to be fully absorbed into self-analysis by American society, its implications include that acts of good will as well as acts of hostility are racist in motive and purpose. Blacks who have not escaped as individuals into white society have always known this, or at least feared it, and to them the proposition has always seemed painfully belated in appearance. For whites, and particularly for students, whose motivational complicity in racism was minimal, the hurt caused by the truth was deep but salutary. Specifically what it meant was that students had been bewitched. Their insight that there is no salvation of oneself without the salvation of others became, perversely, a search for one's own salvation by the use of the plight of others. Blacks felt instinctively that student cooperation in voter registration did more good for the white liberal student than it did for them. At the least, the white liberal student could in time leave the scene while the resident black had the ominous responsibility of staying where he lived and was now registered and facing the challenge of actually voting for change in his situation.

The Student Nonviolent Coordinating Committee, in espousing the separatist meaning of Black Power, did more for student activism than student idealism could ever have done when it forced them to an honest appraisal of their real, as against their pretended, motives for assistance to blacks. The point was driven home, subtly, that an identification with others whose salvation one sought had to be more extensive than many students were yet ready to express. The sheer mechanics of the situation that exposed *students*—that is, people with long summer vacations ending in commitment to return to their campuses—as only a helping group was the outward sign confirming that real identification was not involved. At the very least, this insight escalated the meaning of activism to the point where the search for salvation had to be more authentic to the seekers than the voter registration drive really was. "He saved others, himself he cannot save," the black might have said of the invading student.

In the education afforded by student activism, however, a number of important lessons were learned by participation in the civil rights movement, and they are lessons that new generations of students take as received truths. The civil rights movement was, in a sense, the discovery, incredibly delayed by the chauvinist and distracting anti-Communism of the cold war, that all is not well with America. Specifically, in addition, it convinced the people most interested in change in our society that change was possible, thus giving a continuing source of hope and energy, and that the rot is extensive, thus giving a continuing stimulus and cause. The importance of these lessons, if they are as well learned as they seem to be, is that we shall not have the kind of "peace" in this country which the students' elders seem to want for some time to come.

A still more important lesson was learned, and this is the most important and dangerous of all to the larger society with its large investment in order. It is the lesson that was learned in jail, the lesson that what the law can do to a person is both less and more than was expected. It is less than was expected because none of the shame or guilt which Americans associate with the prisoner was actually felt,

rather a pride and a sense of accomplishment, even when
only vicarious. It is more than was expected because, as is all
too rarely observed, white middle-class Americans actually
have very little to do with the law as it is actually admin-
istered by police and courts. Distance from the law is a fact
of life in the settled sections of American life, and the rude
encounter with it in Southern rural areas showed the children of the middle class that it was really bad. The importance of this is unparalleled in the experiential learning
that has taken place in this country in this decade. It means
that young Americans discovered for themselves that to go
to jail is not the worst thing that can happen to them but
also that people who live close to, not distant from, the law
live lives of unrelieved pain and degradation. If the young
Americans were psychologically alienated, activism in the
civil rights movement helped them to prove that their
alienation was a valid instinct, not a psychological problem,
that there is much in the life of our society to which the only
sane reaction is alienation.

Older liberals have been unnerved by this discovery, at
their peril, for they have known the perfidy of malevolent
law in totalitarian societies and have assumed that the very
definition of our own society, *ipso facto,* included a rejection
of the concept of political crime and the political prisoner.
The radical rejection of liberalism begins with the notion
that this assumption is sanguine. Any society can be driven
to define political crimes, and American society has done
so. That it could do so was demonstrated in the civil rights
movement. That it seems to want to do so has continued
to be demonstrated in the social reaction to a great deal
students have done since. The irony is that the study of the
American revolution richly feeds the growing conviction
among radical students that a political outlaw is what he
really is, and it takes only a little activism to have him

quickly seen as such by those to whom law is sacrosanct. In the debate about what has undermined "law and order" in American life, I would suggest that the culprit is not the anarchic spirit of the young, but the overly legalistic confidence of the rest of us that law, as such, is sacrosanct and can solve all our problems. Students simply do not believe it any more.

The real lesson from the students' failure to effect substantive change in our society on behalf of blacks, from whom they were discovered to be in fact as deeply divided as the rest of society, was to be forced to look to their own expectations for the future. What they saw there was the Selective Service System and the war in Vietnam.

THE NEW PERSPECTIVE ON GOVERNMENT AND NATION

If the civil rights movement fostered the discovery that all was not well with America, the Vietnam war brought about the conviction that all is, in fact, very bad with America. Vigils protesting the war occurred on college campuses following the beginning of the bombing of North Vietnam in 1965, by which time the point of no return in the war had been reached. What began as a merely paternalistic and self-interested advisory program in an Asian country struggling against Communism had become a raging war, using more and more manpower and killing more and more people. Like the history of the black man's struggle, the history of opinion on the Vietnam war demonstrates clearly the great importance of radical opinion in American life; and if nothing else can be said about student radicalism, it now appears beyond dispute that the views thought very radical in 1965 on the subject of the war now appear almost normal. It can be debated whether the radicalism should actually get any credit for bringing about the change in public opinion; the press generally feels that the stridency of student protest activities delayed the development of viable antiwar sentiment in the populace generally. My point here is not to assign or define causation but to observe that the students were again proven right. If it should happen that the Selective Service System itself should be brought to a long overdue end as a result of our Vietnam adventure, the irony (and the tragedy always implicit in irony) will be deeper. In short, what Americans have reacted to most strongly in the content of student activism has gradually become the content of the program espoused by those same Americans. But we still seem altogether too frightened to transcend our American fear of the young, particularly of the student young, and admit this.

The first and essential suspicion about Vietnam that engaged student attention was that "the United States government has been deceptive in its claims of concern for the freedom of the Vietnamese people, just as the government has been deceptive in claiming concern for the freedom of colored people in such other countries as the Dominican Republic, the Congo, South Africa, Rhodesia, and in the United States itself" (from a SNCC statement on the war). This suspicion was expressed in intellectual activities. The function of the teach-in when it was a popular device of dissent was as much study of the war as declamation of our purposes in it. And the study of the war was the most remarkable aspect of the early months of dissent. Students frequently proved their intellectual capacities in the mastery of difficult and complicated sources of information about the war, and in the classical role of the intellectual, raised searching questions about its justification. Such issues as who the Viet Cong actually were, what the extent of our actual service to the people of Vietnam was, what the reasons were for the obvious popularity of Ho Chi Minh, how the American government had lost the congenial relationship with him which it enjoyed at the end of World War II, and so on, were the kind of questions which the teach-in probed and deliberated on. Thus a body of information was built up and circulated among students and other radicals long before it began to appear in the press. It was this study of the war that established the certainty about issues of American foreign policy in Asia that eventually began to be expressed by influential Congressmen and Senators, and gave Senator Eugene McCarthy a ready platform in the presidential primaries of 1968. The importance of noting it here is that it renders ridiculous the antiradical charges of the time which saw student protest and dissent about the war as naïve and innocent. What was neither naïve nor innocent about their protest was the demand that a free society must try to find a better method of pursuing its foreign policy than deceiving its people.

STUDENT ACTIVISM AND THE VIETNAM WAR

The most effective protests against the war in Vietnam have been the mass occasions of demonstration in the major cities. Attention was drawn to the willingness to be counted and hence committed to a policy of open opposition to a firmly established and tirelessly justified policy of the government. It is neither surprise nor secret that the impingement upon students by the Selective Service System, the closest instrument to hand of the war policy, made the draft a primary target for particular kinds of protests. The short-lived fad of burning, or turning in, registration and classification cards ("draft cards") resulted in perhaps the paradigm case in this century of a repressive law defining a purely political crime. Congress's legislation against draft-card burning gave a kind of sacredness to an administrative document which should be reserved at most for the flag.

Can it be surprising that honor to the flag suffers by comparison? The prescription of the Selective Service laws that draft cards be carried on one's person at all times has been interpreted variously by the courts where it has been deliberated, but it was clear to students that it is a form of control by i.d. card and not qualitatively different from other more invidious bureaucratic devices employed to provide ready access to the status of citizens—in other words, a quasi-military rite unfitting in a free society.

Again, the important thing to note in the draft-card-burning frenzy is not the content or character of the act. Had activism reached a more confident level among students, a viable protest would have been to have draft cards burned *en masse* by numbers too great for ordinary legal procedures to deal with. Perhaps that would have been an important turning point. But the significant thing about it is the note of commitment which was now sought by many students whose teach-in participation and group activism had failed to touch the system in the personal way in which it in fact touches them. Some act of protest involving their own participation in the system seemed an important method of commenting upon their evaluation of the system as a whole. As commitment, it had an irreversible and once-for-all effect that is to be noted in all genuine activism.

Students' ideals are relatively open and secure. There is great need for them to explore ways in which activism can provide a commitment commensurate with their ideals. The provision of such commitment is of the essence of protest, demonstration, obstruction, and other activities. Although the following description is somewhat romantic, it captures the meaning as experienced in a hotel demonstration in San Francisco in 1965: "Once inside, one could relax, for one was committed at last in some way to those things one had been told as a child were right and valuable —liberty, justice, equality. Each of us knew at last that he

believed in these things. . . . We each realized . . . that we were not alone. One spent a lifetime in America hedging one's bets, keeping up one's guard, never letting anyone else look too deep, for fear of being laughed at or looking foolish; but we were a thousand strong and each in our own way we knew that we believed, that we all believed." *
This event took place some years ago, and in the context of protest for civil rights, but the same mood has been present whenever large and important protests have occurred. Bets are no longer hedged, commitment becomes irreversible, and confirms what was only belief. Activism against the war in the large protests and in intense study and discussion activity served the same purpose of moving students onto ground from which they could not easily retreat. Activism commits.

Dissent on the war in Vietnam, at first divisive, then spreading widely through the student community, has been clearly a form of the search for salvation. When it has concentrated on the dishonesty and self-interest of American policy in Vietnam, it has equally and clearly been a case of seeing that no salvation for oneself was possible apart from the salvation of others. Vietnam and all it has stood for constitute an impediment to the kind of fulfillment and aspiration which are conditions for salvation. In opposing the war, students chose to participate in the evil endured by the Vietnamese by taking the side of those from whom all choices have been removed rather than performing a blind consent in the crusade against the red peril. Protesting against a policy which removed human choices from large numbers of people, especially when the policy was justified on the ground of making political choice against Communism possible, caused radicals to find them-

* From Paul Jacobs and Saul Landau (eds.), *The New Radicals: A Report with Documents* (New York: Random House, 1966), pp. 213–214.

selves in a more than superficial identification with this world's sufferers. Their own choices were diminished. It is the ease with which radical activism has been able to create for the white liberal student situations in which he is treated in derogatory ways by established authority that has been a chief factor in "radicalization." To a great extent opponents of the war have experienced the crushing frustration and hopelessness of standing up against a relentless, self-righteous American government which other peoples have known all too long. At home, the blacks sat out the Chicago Democratic Convention protests in 1968 for the most part, arguing that it was time the student radicals found out just what it was like to bear the brunt of police reaction. Thus "radicalization" comes to mean finding oneself regarded by one's society in the same ways one's society regards outsiders to it; and when thus radicalized, one begins to see all that is being done in one's name. And when it begins to be done to oneself, an effective identification with others to whom it is routinely done has come about. A solution has been found to the charge made by black militants to white liberals, "You don't get radicalized fighting other people's battles" (Gloria Steinem in *New York* magazine, April 7, 1969); but the solution lies only in the genuine act of making other people's causes truly your own.

Thus there arose for activism the necessity to focus on the Selective Service System as a target, because conformity with the draft imposed on the young complicity in American policy as focused in Vietnam. Nowhere more clearly than in Selective Service did students find that their own choices were effectively narrowed and in many cases removed from them by the requirements of military service, and that as long as they complied, they were supporters of a policy they increasingly despised.

I have not yet seen equanimity toward Selective Service

among students. Students will go to any lengths in their plans to deal with the impending doom of the draft—including ROTC and programs of officer training—in the hope of avoiding the removal of choice. Until the end of graduate-student deferments in 1968, "doing something about the draft" was not necessarily a selfish, and certainly not a cowardly, course of action, when a way of avoiding the draft for oneself was not difficult to find. Some witness against the system that produced the manpower for the Vietnam War, and operated unequally and severely against young men unable to avoid the draft through education, was required, even if it resulted in placing the student in more, rather than less, personal danger.

The resistance stimulated, with the aid of the American Friends Service Committee, widespread consideration of conscientious objection, a time-honored and legal, but previously not socially acceptable, way out of required military service. The tortuous definitions of "religious training and belief" required of young men from the nonserious mainline churches and synagogues, and the intransigence of countless local boards and State appeal boards to manifestly just claims to objector classification, made this route treacherous. The logic of conscientious objection, moreover, virtually requires eventual disobedience of the Selective Service law when the claim has been turned down at every level and military induction is ordered, since either the sincerity or the sanity of the conscientious objector is called into question if he changes his mind as represented in his statements on the CO form and accepts induction. Acceptance of induction is *prima facie* evidence of his insincerity. Not only is it the case that many students have investigated the possibility that they are conscientious objectors only to find the stakes much higher than any evidence for traditional religious conviction can justify, but many have also rejected a system the essential feature of which seems self-defeating: the labeling of an act as conscientious, and the judging of that act by others, not oneself. *Conscience* is a supremely personal and individual concept. The Selective Service Act, however, defines conscientious objection as valid only when based on some religious belief other than "a merely personal code"—a contradiction that seems to have been lost not only on the administrators of the draft but on Congress as well. The contradictions and anomalies in conscientious objection have made it a possible course of draft resistance for only the hardiest, and because of the inefficiency of the system, a successful course only for the luckiest.

Refusal of induction into the armed services, whether after a prior attempt at securing conscientious-objector classification or not, is another form of draft resistance taken up by the individual in circumstances of loneliness so acute as only to be compared to that experienced by the unwilling soldier himself; by such action the individual opposes the entire philosophy of conscription in the only way open to him in a law-laden culture: disobedience. The loneliness cannot be much alleviated by the supportive alienation of large numbers of clergy and others who proclaim their intellectual and moral complicity in the disobedience of resisters.

THE DISCOVERY OF PASSIVE PROTEST

To dwell on draft resistance and conscientious objection as forms of activism may be bewildering to some, but it should be observed that *not doing* is as important a form of activism as *doing*. We shall see later that along with increased activism of various kinds among students, there has been an increased refusal to act in ways that society seems to require, and that both act and refusal have arisen from the same motive. Protest against the Vietnam war has taken many forms, but perhaps none is socially as important as these forms of the activism of *not doing*, of refusing, in some manner, to comply with the system. "Suppose they gave a war and nobody came," is still only a dream, but it is closer to reality than it has ever been before.

Active protest against the war has been made, moreover, more credible by various forms of passive protest against it. This confirms our earlier insight that one cannot merely seek salvation for others by some arbitrary or artificial identification with the oppressed but must seek some authentic means of genuine identification by seeing that what one's society does in one's name and with one's compliance is done either by oneself or to oneself. In seeking what may seem a merely selfish escape for oneself from the inhuman and peremptory removal of choices which Selective Service represents, the other, more powerful, conviction is expressed that there is no salvation for oneself apart from the salvation of others.

Despite the loneliness of disobedience, a community of activism emerges with a telling denunciation of the militarism of modern society, a denunciation which saves more than its own members. This community says that what society does will not be done by any agency within the community's realm of choices and demonstrates its sincerity by opening itself to what society will do *to* it. In legal, social, and historical terms, it may well fail, for it invites a chauvinist backlash from what Dan Wakefield has called "Supernation." In moral terms, its conviction is unassailable. Put starkly, it is better to be killed than to kill. Those who are willing so to simplify the issues in order to lay hold on some kind of salvation will likely be killed, if only by being done to death in argument with their more cautious peers, bored to death by the insouciant self-righteousness of their elders, or chewed into ineffectiveness by the complex, lumbering, and impersonal enterprise of American jurisprudence to which they expose themselves. Hopefully they will not lose the sound of their drummer.

Thus the twin problems of racism and war have evoked activist response liberalizing large numbers of students, radicalizing a smaller but still remarkably significant number of others; and although activism in both areas has failed to accomplish its purpose of relieving the problems, lessons have been learned in both. Negatively, the chief lesson is that no one can live peacefully in an unexamined society in the modern world for no human institution can be trusted to function as it was intended to function. Positively, the chief lesson has been the discovery of *courage* in facing down the anomalies in our social life which impede the process of becoming human. Courage is a loaded word which can mask arrogance and myopia as well as implement virtue or value. Part of our social turmoil is simply the newness of the display of courage in taking on the system in an age when the individual feels helpless to influence his world. Courage is dangerous and gives rise to combat and, at the same time, makes caution a temptation. Until the courageous manner and the idealistic matter of student unrest come together, many mistakes are inevitable, and incomprehension at unrest by those who are at rest will be unavoidable. In taking on both racism and war students more and more have learned that courage is not for the rare and mythic hero alone, but for oneself.

THE CRITICISMS OF ACTIVISM

The common criticisms of student activism as seen in demonstrations, protest marches, sit-ins, war and draft resistance rallies and literature, and opposition to various aspects of the political process as it works in America are so misguided as to be dangerous. It is not surprising that activism so criticized has matured in seriousness and concreteness into the student revolution which will be examined later. The criticisms indicate that the integrity and sincerity of the activities have not been believed by the rest of the society. To see activism, for example, as a rebellion against parents that has been projected onto society as a whole is an analysis that is not psychiatrically proven or even strongly indicated in studies that have attempted to arrive at a social-psychological explanation for student unrest. There is still the usual amount of generational conflict in college students, but at worst it takes the form of cynical pity toward fathers rather than rage. At best, and more often, among radical students there appears an admiration of fathers, a sign that these students are already past adolescent hostility and hence prematurely adult as against the traditional pattern.

Similarly the criticisms of student activism on the grounds that it is all negative, that no program to take the place of what is attacked as evil is ever suggested, or that students do not know enough to grasp the critical attacks on activism, amount to nothing but an unlovely adult *hubris*. When activist explorations of injustice arise, it is by definition that they arise in situations where others, elders, have the control of resources and responsibility for structures out of which programs are made. To propose alternatives to escalation of the war in Vietnam or to *de facto* racism in housing or employment practices would be to indulge in abstractions that would be attacked as unrealistic and impossible. Numberless committees in American institutions have responded to activist criticism that what was offered as solution was too vague to be dealt with and that a specific program should be proposed instead, only to respond to the specific program with the assertion that it was so detailed as to require basic policy decisions that the committee in question was not empowered to make. It is a virtue that the students generally have not been snowed by the criticism that they have no alternatives to offer for that which they attack but have been satisfied that their negativism was a right and necessary prelude to change. If attack succeeds, responsibility will be shifted and control of resources realigned and new, hopefully more humane, programs will be created. To be required to say beforehand what they will be is to be asked the impossible. To require alternative structures of student activists is to be more than accidentally dishonest, or else naïve, about how social structures and programs come into being.

Perhaps the least serious criticism of student activism is that it is all done for publicity—that leaders of student demonstrations and protests are concerned for their own image and renown. This is an unfortunate criticism in two ways. One, it is essential in a society like our own that communication of views be efficiently and widely accomplished. There is no point in mounting a protest against a war from a hermit's cave, if the hope is to have some effect on the war. Publicity for protest is a part of protest and the gift for "getting publicity" is essential to the success of protest. It is a trivial criticism that it is the publicity that is wanted. There is no other way to make one's protest known in this celebrity-bound world. Manipulation of media is a central fact of genuine radical activism. The other way in which this criticism is unfortunate is related to what we have already observed, that the publicity machine is controlled and manipulated by other than students. The press, not hippies, destroyed hippies. The press, not activists, distorts activist motives. A look at the underground press will convince such a critic of what student radicals really have in mind in the field of publicity.

The chief adult criticism has taken the form of assuming that students should be protected from error. The criticism is that the greater experience and familiarity with pitfalls which inform the wisdom of society's managers alone can prevent the idealism and courage of the young from falling into error. Such paternalism fails to get the most elementary point of activism: that colossal error is exposed and proclaimed in that analysis of society which activism nourishes, that there are no greater errors possible than racism and war. The implication that the young can be preserved from error by those responsible for American society, even by their silence, is simply absurd. Rhetorically, perhaps more errors of a less horrendous kind are needed.

SOME JUSTIFIED CRITICISMS

The justified criticisms of student activism are more serious. *First,* that despite the increase of activism in the latter half of the sixties, so many students are still students of the fifties—docile, compliant, individualistic, career-oriented, silent. I have tried to show earlier that they are no less angry, and that the system within which they live and work is no less irrelevant to their real aspirations than it is to the radicals. The worst thing to observe about them is that they have not yet begun to learn the lesson of courage, which is another way of saying that they have not yet seen the depth and pain of the blight to which their future careers may contribute rather than correct. They want to "make it," to use the obscene term elevated by Norman Podhoretz into a liberal way of life. Silent students are swallowing their anger in the interests of individual survival, taking, as the society at large does, the ideals of their heritage with something less than full seriousness. The "maturity" of realizing the inevitable gap between ideals and reality impresses them, but this is a self-fulfilling realization. It never accomplishes anything but buying time for the present, which is illusory. Worse, they are turning their backs on the salvation of others in the crudest way, seeking no necessary identification, even of the artificial sort which is better than none, with those who suffer. The mindless dimension of the silent majority is its unawareness that to avoid participating in decisions and actions of one's world is to support them. My point here is that if responsibility for such actions were clear to the individual student, the actions might well be very different than they are.

The use of the fact that only a minority of students are activist as a source of comfort by those who expect the current student unrest to pass is patently dangerous, not least in the sense that we may be experiencing a "last, best hope" for humanizing our culture. To wish it away might cause us to lose it altogether. To use the fact to justify hard measures to put down activism in the current "law and order" mood of those who fear student activism is invidious and even more dangerous. I have observed that students tend to be more like each other than like their elders in their view of the relation between ideal and act, thought and behavior. To attack the minority with repression will result in its translation into a majority of students. This is, again, radicalization, and it has happened too often to be misunderstood. The danger to the settled society is obvious. The danger to student radicalism is that it will develop faster than it has resources to build with. This implies the second criticism.

Second, student activism can be sharply criticized for its not maturing clearly and rapidly enough in bringing together the content of activist anger and the methods of activist programs. (This is not a more subtle form of the old saw about "respecting their goals but not approving their methods," which is a common criticism of little value since there are no approved methods for attacking a social system as such. It is not merely racism and war *in* American society that is to be attacked but racism and war *as* American society, which means that mere dissent is useless.) What this criticism points to is that "student power" is in its infancy in the sense that the interpretation of the methods of activism is not yet fully elaborated to the point where the goals of an activist stance or program are obvious to all observers. Student power does not yet have the unity implied in the draft-resistance motto, "We won't go."

If I were writing solely as a prophet of doom, I would observe that student power has not yet even definitely appeared, but that when it does appear it will endanger every institution in our society, not excluding the family. Since my purpose is to attempt a useful understanding of what students are doing today, I put this as a challenge to those students who have leadership within the student community: there has to be a continuing analysis of student power as a medium to the point where it can become clear whether "the medium is the message." Not until that happens can control and responsibility be shared by those whose aspirations are still uncloyed by their careers. This may be unreconstructed "Old Left" speaking, but it seems to me that for every confrontation that takes place in student activism, there should be a lot of closed door, secret, and completely candid talk sessions emanating in further definitions of student power as a means of allowing thought to grow with action. The instinct of black militants in closing many of their activities to any white observers is a valid instinct which students tend to shun. They do so, admirably, in the name of honesty and candor. But they are not being heard to mean what they say, and they should work harder at developing a theory of student power at the same time that sample tests of it are appearing.

Third, student activism can be criticized for its selection of issues. Civil rights activism in its earlier form died a necessary death, and the protests against the war in Vietnam took its place. Valiant efforts, at this writing, are still made to keep that issue alive, but the continuing prosecution of the war after the illusion of hope appeared in peace talks has had an enervating effect. In addition, the pressing of numerous legal cases related to opposition to the war and civil disobedience has occupied the attention and energy of activists in a form that has suspended activity pending judgment. That this should have been expected and that it has really nothing to do with the real program of activism have not been thoroughly considered by students. The paucity of student activity relative to the Nigeria-Biafra conflict, the placid American involvement in South African *apartheid,* and the commercial complicity in air and water pollution—all "recognized" issues—is unfortunate. Cynically, it might be said there are enough problems to keep students activist all the time. Less cynically, the search for the real issue has turned haltingly and sometimes incredulously to the educational institution itself. Here it becomes a real problem of relevance and then of revolution, and here the search for salvation has finally arrived where it belongs, on the site of the lives which students actually live in the present. My criticism is that it has taken so long to arrive, and the importance of the criticism is that students may tire of it or lose heart before some real path to salvation is discovered in time.*

* For confirmation of much of the preceding argument, see "Reflections on Youth Movements," by Walter Laqueur, in *Commentary,* June, 1969.

THE SALVATION IN ACTIVISM

I have contended that activism is saving in several steps; that contrary to interior programs of individual salvation or the search for communities within the larger society wherein the negative dimensions of the larger society can be ignored, activism represents the discovery that salvation for oneself is not possible apart from salvation of others. In civil rights activism it was discovered that this must not be perverted into the notion that salvation can be sought for others with whom one is only artificially identified. In war protest, in the activism both of doing and refusing to do, was found a field in which activism brought an authentic identification of one's own salvation from the system with the salvation of others from the oppressions of the system. And finally, that the complicity of the university itself, as a paradigm of society, makes it the real, though heretofore latent, object of anger and protest previously directed elsewhere.

Avenues to salvation have been explored in activism in the sense of attempts to rectify errors in one's own society— relieving oppression, redressing injustice, ending suffering, or alleviating it at least, and honoring humanity. Merely to have attempted these things is saving, but, paradoxically, at the same time activism has not been saving in that nothing has been accomplished. America is still racist, still at war, and, in the latter case, will end the war, if it does, out of self-interest and not out of genuine concern for humanity. Activism has failed because there is no place, apparently, to get at American society, no place yet discovered where the disease is more than on the surface. My image is that of an elephant pricked with pins here and there in its skin, sometimes deeply enough and seriously enough to be felt, but not really affected organically by the attack. To have failed to affect it at one point has seemed to mean that it should be attacked at another, and so on; and no attack has felled the beast. Activism has been salvific in purpose but not in accomplishment. Individuals have been "saved," but the society remains hell-bent.

6

INTERLUDE ON RELEVANCE: ITS INDISPENSABILITY

When do we live, that's what I'd like to know . . .
—Prerevolutionary student in the film *If.* . . .

Racism, poverty, and war are problems of the whole society and not specifically germane to the college campus. When students become involved in activities directed against racist institutions of the society and against the war, they are introducing into the serene and detached academic life concerns irrelevant to that life. And when they discover that their activities in opposition to racism and war fail, that their ideals have no influence on society at large, this irrelevance is turned around: their lives and hopes are irrelevant to society. The ambiguity of the concept of relevance makes clarity difficult; the "over-kill" employment of the term by students and others makes it seem a rather trite concept. Nevertheless, one of the indispensable preconditions of any search for salvation and one of the never-varying attitudes of students is a pressure for relevance. The adult society belittles this as shallow or naïve. It is time that it was taken seriously.

We have already seen the problem of relevance for the student within the academic framework: that education proceeds on two tracks, one on which a program is conducted by the faculty and administration according to the purposes which the particular institution sets for itself, the other on which students live and on which their "real" education takes place. The two worlds built along these respective tracks have almost nothing to do with each other. To the student, much of what the faculty and administration do most of the time is irrelevant; to the faculty, only what students do academically is of relevance; to the administration, what students do is only negatively relevant, that is attention is only attracted when rules and regulations are broken. Many counselors are marginal to the educational scheme, and also ambiguous. Paid by the institutions for the most part and functioning on behalf of the institution, they help students let off steam or bring personal synthesis of sorts to those individuals least able to cope with the greater irrelevance of the system themselves. For such individuals they meet real needs and, where they are effective, head off the merely pathological reaction to institutional irrelevance experienced by students. More than a few of such counselors, sympathetic with the pathological dangers which the system contains for students not otherwise in need, must wonder whether the function they perform ought to be performed, whether rather another kind of solution to the problem of irrelevance might appear if their function were not present. There is a certain Big Brother dimension to the idea of a huge and complex social institution such as the educational establishment providing built-in therapy for those of its clientele whom it destroys. It is perhaps the most deadening form of repressive tolerance.

What the Demand for Relevance Means

Students generally no longer accept as a necessary evil the irrelevance of the educational community. Their demand for relevance is to bring the two tracks together in the expectation that they can "live" in the collegiate years, not merely prepare to live. In the case of student activism directed at social problems, the demand is that these problems should, as problems, be brought onto the campus, debated, discussed and hopefully solved. There should be disadvantaged students on the campus so that the advantaged students can begin *now* to learn how to deal with them. There should be more blacks on white campuses *now* so that the problem of racism can be *relevantly* faced. The "military-industrial complex" should be recognized as having the same influence on the campus as on society generally (a point about which college administrators have been generally deceptive) in order that the issues it presents can be realistically dealt with. If one's posture has become antimilitaristic, then military elements on the campus, such as ROTC programs, must be recognized for what they are. In some cases, the demand for relevance has involved bringing onto the campus elements of the social realities of our life from which the campus has hitherto been artificially protected, such as urban social problems. In others, the demand has required the recognition of social, nonacademic elements of our life which have been permitted a masked presence on the campus because of some ancillary benefaction to the institution which they brought, such as government research contracts.

It may be that in a complex society, even one that encourages its citizens to be strongly individualistic and to imagine themselves genuinely influential, relevance is ruled out by definition, or relegated to those efforts we all make to create our own world-within-the-world, where the relevance of things is within our power to determine. Such hopelessness has not been successfully bred into our present generations of college age and under. The interdependence of men on men throughout the world, an impossible dream to the settled society, has become an assumption for the unsettled young. Their insight is that unless there is relevance in their studies and their living *now,* there will not be any society in which to enjoy one's long-sought maturity or salvation. With a Vietnam in the offing for any student, this is not merely melodramatic. "Business as usual" for the traditional academic institution has run up against the harshly apocalyptic intuition that the fundamental sin is to accept what one of Ignazio Silone's characters speaks of as temporary living. "We all live temporary lives. . . . We think that just for now things are going badly, that we have to adapt just for now, and even humiliate ourselves, but that all this is temporary. Real life will start someday." * The intuition, in the words of a characteristic graffito, is that "today is the first day of the rest of your life!"

As long as students were able to regard college merely as a puberty rite or simply as a place, and to direct their concern for relevance at the problems of the society into which they were preparing to move after graduation, campus authorities allowed and even warmly encouraged the activism directed at the world outside. But together with the repeated proof of the inefficacy of that activism, caused by our society's almost inexhaustible capacity to absorb dissent without responding to it, came the belated discovery that the campus was not all that detached from the rest of society but was a microcosm of it. As a problem of relevance, this was the discovery that the task was not simply to bring the moral pressure of the prestigious intellectual world of the campus to bear on the society—a comparatively easy task—but to expose the complicity of the educational world in buttressing and expanding a society increasingly irrelevant to the aspirations of the young. This is to expose an even more basic disparity within the educational structure

* *Bread and Wine* (New York: Atheneum, 1962), p. 43.

than the academic disparity of education along two tracks implied. The university was discovered to be "them" not "us." The task is to make it "us" not "them." The university, precisely because it is *not* serene and detached, becomes the object of student activism, and activism becomes a kind of revolution. The problem of relevance, then—present, gestating, and unsolved for a very long time on the campus—has afforded the students transition from a laudable idealism directed at problems all liberals want solved (or so they say) to an angry, sometimes arrogant opposition to the very society in which they live, that of the educational institution. The student's world, he has finally discovered, is the college. There is no hope for society becoming "relevant" until the college itself becomes so.

The Issue of Black Studies

"Black studies" has been the most widely pressed issue that is justified in the name of relevance, and is hence the most likely to throw light on the problem of relevance as it affects all students. In an effort to offer in justice its benefits to those in society most in need of them, institutional attempts to increase the number of black students in their student bodies have proliferated to the point where "qualified" black students can practically name their college and the less "qualified" enter programs of upgrading and remedial work. In either case, the number of black students has increased dramatically on previously white campuses. I will not here enter into the problem suggested by my use of "qualified" except to agree with those who say the issue is not one of simple qualification but precisely the problem of the irrelevance of our testing and admissions and qualification procedures for most black youth. Remedial work is long overdue on the qualification process not only on the people who are excluded by it.

Black students have found the traditional college curriculum specifically and generally irrelevant to their needs
and aspirations as well as largely incommunicable to their
backgrounds. The discovery of black pride has not been
well served by the nearly complete absence of opportunity
to confirm that pride in solid historical, literary, and religious studies which white men control. The media of communication—music, poetry, talk, dance—which express
black life are as authentic as the media traditionally associated with white academia: prose, lectures, European music,
ballet. When black students make demands for black
studies, it is as much the media of communication that are
at issue as the content of courses. An aspect of this question apparently not widely understood is that white students' support of this demand is not altogether altruistic
or, what is thought to be worse, a kind of pragmatic revolutionary alliance. White students sense that blacks have a
more just and demonstrable claim for increased relevance
in the work they are asked to do in college, but that the
securing of that claim will have a good effect on the relevance of courses and work white students are asked to do
also.

The traditional departmental divisions of academic study
—chopped-up bits of the world to be synthesized, if at all,
by the ingenious student in his solitude—are irrelevant in
the extreme to the black student whose experience has been
holistic and entire—that he is black has been the common
denominator of all his experience in America. If he can
succeed in demanding approaches to knowledge that are as
holistic and multidepartmental as his experience, the white
student will have gained much as well. The fine depart-
mentalization of studies is of interest only to those whites
desiring the most meticulous reproduction in themselves
of their favorite teachers; to most white students the divisions of knowledge are as inimical as they are to blacks,

if for a slightly different reason. Their experience has been holistic also, although not directed to such a factor as race; their experience has been holistic in its healthy self-centeredness. Sociological and historical factors have allowed white young people to label this as "individuality" while blacks have had to experience it as "blackness." It is the same experience qualitatively, and the fragmented, increment-accruing college curriculum is equally irrelevant to each. What blacks are finally in a position to fight for, whites will do well to assist in securing, and perhaps both, after the smoke settles, will have begun to explore what is the clearly implied question in the demands of each: what it is, again, to be wholly human.

Let me be emphatic that I see the black studies debate as a paradigm of the whole question of the relevance of education to students, not because to settle it would answer all the problems but because to settle it properly would be to rearrange a great many priorities in education for whites as well as blacks. Black studies is as important an issue in the further problems it implies for interdepartmental intellectual life as any other issue on the campus. To bolster white support for it is my intention, not to pontificate as to its proper course. Black students will, in pressing their claim, do many things that the white institution will never understand, and which will hurt the *status quo* badly. Whites can show more grace than to mask their own fears in critical analysis or attempt a continued white domestication of blackness by pretending to have all the answers.

THE ISSUE OF AUTHORITY

Another case of irrelevance appears in the whole realm of authority. Authority as such is not the object of student rebellion, for there are aspects of authority that are invulnerable. What is attacked is formal authority. Analysis of authority used to proceed on the distinction between *imperium* and *auctoritas,* which refer, roughly, to power vs. authorship, the muscular vs. the spiritual. One is the kind of authority which an authority figure simply has, the other is the kind he deserves. *Imperium* never bothers to commend itself, *auctoritas* never has to defend itself. The formal authority of college administrators and of some faculty, *imperium,* is obviously under serious attack. *Auctoritas* tends to be the authority of leadership, charisma, and influence, or the hero model which leads, or at least brings about, the attack. To attack *imperial* authority is in the American grain, even though we have depersonalized this formal type of authority into the abstract concept of law. The uneven ministrations of the law, while not an argument for anarchy, are a strong influence toward the necessary re-examination of the nature of authority by students, and the realignment of allegiances. *Imperium* can command obedience, but it will not soon again command the respect of students. *Auctoritas* may seem to the rest of society to be chaotic and, for a time, anarchistic, but it is the type of authority out of which loyalty and commitment arise. We err if we take pride in the depersonalization of authority without taking great care to see that the authority of law is not merely imperial authority. In educating vast numbers of our young on the college level, we open all merely formal authority to a devastating scrutiny which it cannot survive.

The Morality Impasse

This is perhaps best to be seen in the *morality impasse* between students and the rest of us. The students tend to search for moral strength within the context of a personal freedom that is attentive to avoiding the occasions of pain for others. By contrast, at least in the students' view, the rest of society, when it speaks of morals, means only personal morality. To translate this into categories, students generally feel that the authorities under which they live in college regard morality as chiefly a matter of drugs and sex at the expense of race, poverty, and war. When discussions take place on morality, students and their elders are likely to be talking about two different worlds entirely. What students are seeking is personal commitment in the social sphere, while adults seem to wish that students would be more attentive to social pressures upon the individual in his privacy. To each, the moral concerns of the other are irrelevant. In the context of our thesis, it is central to the search for salvation that a viable morality be worked out. To students the emphasis is upon the social sins rather than the individual improprieties. In their view, inattention to the social problems of our country, foreign and domestic, relieves the authority figures from any right to legislate about the private morality of students. And to proclaim their view, some "go public" in the areas of hair, dress (and undress), and obscenity. The secrecy with which problems of private morality are dealt with by the larger society is accurately despised for what it is, a hypocrisy.

What this all means for the question of the relevance of authority is that students are not seeking so much to replace one authority with another or to defy authority generally, but to label certain areas as beyond or outside the scope of the authorities altogether. It is *imperium* which is frightened by such a demand.

THE PEDAGOGICAL IMPASSE

Another, and much more significant, dimension of the problem of relevance which can only be suggested here, for it deserves lengthy and careful study by itself, is the *pedagogical impasse* that is implied in the role of experience in learning. Much of the educational world is irrelevant to precisely those for whose benefit it is designed, the students, because they have come to accept, decades after its introduction to educational philosophy, the indispensability of experience in learning and growth. One of the chief reasons for the widening of the cultural gap between students and their teachers over the past decade is the increasing variety of experiences from which students have learned about themselves, and from which they have learned the importance of ideas and insights talked about, but not experienced, in the classroom and lecture hall.

Pedagogically, it is the final impact of the scientific method on other areas of education, for in laboratory courses it has never been seriously questioned that experiencing the concept dealt with is necessary for full understanding. Experience and experiment, after all, are from the same root. The unplanned effect of the drama of science on other fields of academic work has been to extend the necessity of experiencing to fields that have traditionally been merely conceptual or intellectual—the extension of the notion of experiencing into perception, feeling, and performance. Philosophy has responded positively to this influence for some time in its method of "doing" its discipline rather than merely hearing about it. Poetry and other kinds of creativity, however, have been less successful in producing practitioners of their disciplines than in developing criticism, and it may be criticism is the consummate irrelevance. Students in everything from film-making to yoga to sensitivity training have been exploring the world of experience with an avidity their teachers would desire in more narrowly intellectual pursuits. Obviously this is one result also of the "media explosion" and the wider varieties of perception to which present college students have been exposed from infancy, and it is the new level at which education must be organized in the future. It also means that students feel themselves uninvolved in education as they encounter it. At the same time, they have become aware of their capability in educating one another, which undermines the *imperium* of traditional scholarship and teaching more than we realize.

A possible rebuttal here would be that students are short-sighted when they allow any of these examples to be elevated into the cry of irrelevance as they do. It could be argued that taking up any new course of study or any new style of life, both of which are clearly demanded by growth and the increase of wisdom, is to venture into the "irrelevant." It is to expose oneself to the unknown, the unexperienced, that which is not in one's background, and that which, for a time, one has to accept "on authority" as one moves, hopefully, toward the discovery of its relevance. The argument would imply that students lack humility and that they may even be afraid of what their elders possess that is new to them at their age. But students who are experimenting in the manner that students are doing today cannot be described as afraid of the unknown or cautious in the face of the new. It is the known of which they are afraid, the outrageous world which the wisdom of the ages has produced.

SANCTUARY FOR WHAT?

A final ambivalence in the question of relevance must be noted. In the catalog of campus unrest in the spring of 1969, one university board of trustees is quoted thus: "The university is not a sanctuary from the law" (*The New York Times,* May 2, 1969). In one sense this is exactly what campus rebellions are about, and students would add, "nor from anything else this world presents." The indispensability of relevance requires that the campus no longer be thought a sanctuary at all, and it is by no means clear that students want this to be the case any more than administrators and faculty. But if the managers of the campus feel themselves the wiser in the current debate, it would seem to be incumbent on them to strive for consistency. Most student activities in search of salvation tend to be ridiculed by faculty and administrators because they are not relevant to the purposes of the institution and the traditions of higher education. They are importations onto the campus of attitudes and values inappropriate to reasoned discourse and the pursuit of the truth. Curiously, however, where social attitudes on personal morality, such as with drugs and sex, are concerned, it is precisely in the name of the standards of the outside world that intervention into the serenity of the campus is defended. When the question is unruliness or even violence, most campus authorities would not even think of it as intervention, but begin thinking of their rebelling students as "them" not "us."

Students wish to make their college life more relevant if only because it may be the last life they will lead. The demand for consistency upon students is that they accept the anomaly and ambiguity of the campus in our society for now but continue to work toward its renovation. What they must accept is the panic they arouse in the American public, and calculate whether the consequences of their programs are worth what they are going to cost. If the question were put baldly, "Are police relevant to the campus?" students would surely say No. But it should be understood that what they are saying is that police are not "relevant" to society at all, which is to say that the authority of law as it is used in America—to assist an immoral war, to "investigate" the poor, and to maintain the racist *status* *quo*—is no longer what law was intended to be, or yet ought to be. A counsel of perfection? Yes, but where else are such fundamental questions of cultural purpose appearing? *

If I am right in seeing the demand for relevance, and the other aspects of the student mood today, as a search for salvation, it means that there is a seriousness in students' activities which may yet transcend individual fears and the more physical of society's threats. It means also that if they fail, it may be the last chance at anything like salvation they will get. It is not in the least surprising that students, by way of the things they are doing today, have arrived at the point of seeking salvation through revolution.

* The Honorable C. J. Wyzanski, in *U.S. v. Sisson,* has argued that the moral force of the law depends upon its capacity reasonably to express the community's highest morality.

7

SALVATION THROUGH REVOLUTION

> And so you ask, "What about the innocent bystanders?"
> But we are in a time of revolution. If you are a by-
> stander, you are not innocent.
>
> —Free

To call what is going on among students a "revolution" is
no longer hyperbole. Activism, however saving, is simply
not a decisive enough word to describe the disruptions of
normal campus activity that have caused the newspapers to
keep front-page box scores, and the nightly newscasts to
allow the campus to displace the war for prime coverage.
The search for salvation to which students are committed
in the various ways that have been described has become
relevant in the extreme in being focused on the educational
institution itself. It has increased dramatically in seriousness to the point where "revolution" has become the terrifying but unavoidable word for it. Our task is to continue
to see whether the model of the search for salvation serves
to give any useful explanation of what students are doing
and, by it, to come to an understanding of this revolution.
Perhaps we can discover a corrective for the fact that we
have long made the mistake of using the word "revolution"
too loosely at the same time as we have taken the fact of
revolution altogether too lightly. Because of this, society

at large and the educational establishment in particular are strangely hurt and surprised, and angered, by the beginnings of literal revolution, and tend further to polarize the revolutionary ideals of students.

REVOLUTION AND THE UNIVERSITY

Revolution has begun, by anyone's definition, when tactical violence begins to appear. Blacks have rightly insisted that "rebellion" rather than "riot" is the name of the urban explosions which have marked their recognition of the futility of nonviolence and their challenge to the rest of America that they are serious in their demands. Yet substantive change rather than violence is the essence of revolution, and we do not err when we conceive of peaceful revolutions. The precise character of violence in the American self-image is much discussed and still not widely recognized. The violence of the black revolution and of the student revolution provide one more opportunity for studying, and admitting, the trust in violence which they see as characteristic of American life. Thus I see it as tactical violence whose chief purpose is to draw out the violence of the establishment in its self-defense. For, in fact, the violence that succeeds, loses. And one thing that is abundantly clear to those in revolution in America is that if they press their claims with consistent violence, they will be defeated with the greater power of the state. Any serious revolution in this country can be put down easily, if force is the only issue. Violence (as well as the threat of it on the part of those in revolution) is serious and determined, but its purpose is to draw out the innate violence of the elements of control in society and in the university so that they might be seen to be the kind of authority they are, *imperium,* not *auctoritas.*

A nonviolent protest has the disadvantage of being possible to be written off as not important, empty of real commitment, the protesters not meaning what they say. A club or a gun tends to mean what it says in America, and the response of greater, more serious violence is quickly drawn. Such a response is most clearly drawn when the university turns over to the outside society its security and safety and proves that when the chips are down it desires identification with the *status quo,* rather than with progress and change. The response of violence which the university makes in order to get back to the business of "reasoned discourse" makes it the loser. Where this is a clearcut result, more students are radicalized and greater change is imminent.

The more dependent on force the university is for its survival the more clearly does it prove itself incapable of performing its real function, and in the eyes of students it is the weakness of the educational institution, rather than its strength, that is being displayed. The crisis of trust in education which this implies is likely to be decisive. The extreme will arrive when it is discovered that students as such are "them" for the university as they are for much of American society. There will be very little left of the traditions of education on which to build a new society.

The question is not that such a disaster is likely to occur as a result of revolution. The question is whether the revolutionaries are to blame for it and, being defined as a minority unapproved of by their fellow students, should be excised from the college scene before they have their way. And this question is being addressed in ways that will surely exacerbate, not solve, the problem posed by revolution. It is being assumed that student revolutionaries are responding to some agreed master plan for disrupting the universities when in fact the conclaves at which "the revolution" is discussed are disorganized and even chaotic, and in an organization like SDS the individual chapters are so autonomous as to make many observers wonder how it survives. Within individual chapters, further fragmentation of views makes the situation even less conspiratorial. The revolution, even in its literal and violent episodes, is spontaneous and dependent on factors arising from local situations and the availability of talents for leadership that vary from place to place in the country. It is here, moreover, that those concerned must continually remind themselves that student unrest is not an American, or even a Western, phenomenon, but has appeared in all the major countries of the world. Applauding the unrest of Soviet students while imagining a Communist conspiracy informing the unrest of American students is simply ridiculous. The moral authority of the university is effectively abandoned when it fails to cry out against the legislators' desire to approach the problem on a conspiratorial theory when everyone associated with the college scene knows how continuous is the spectrum from mild dissent or indifference through vocal antagonism and specific activism to the taking over of buildings and other disruptions. The fact is that the revolution is *more serious* than a conspiratorial theory allows. The extent of alienation and the potential for radicalization is all the greater for the spontaneity and selectivity of student activism, and we are in grave danger of not realizing how little of the iceberg has actually appeared. The logical extreme of the repressive approach is an educational institution without its best students present at all. A more likely result is drearier: a university system catering only to career-dominated training programs, with no vestige left of the classical goal of education in meditation on the meaning of being human.

The revolution, at all the levels at which it appears, is

directed against the institution as institution, in the name of an educational ideal of an institution as community, as people, and consequently the administration of education is the primary target. Teachers are vulnerable in their having forfeited genuine responsibility for the educational community to managers, since within the educational world learning is a credential for acceptable authority. Whether the ideal can be achieved in the context of American education, where size and universality have become values, is the question posed by the revolution. The result could be a revision of our system of regarding the college degree as a proof of maturity (the end of the puberty rite). Or it could be the destruction of educational institutions which refuse to act like the living human communities they are called to be. In either case, it is a challenge to our present concepts of educational authority and relevance, and it is the institution as such, not education as such, which is attacked. To indulge in rhetoric about the dangers which revolutionaries present to the genuine educative functions of the institutions they disrupt is to assume that these functions are being performed. The students' revolutionary claim is that they are not—as long as the institution remains a complacent and contributing participant in a society that has no apparent humane goals. The revolution, therefore, may be the only relevant effort being made to *save* education and thus create a community in which the search for salvation can be fed by any real kind of hope.

We can understand and assist the necessary revolution only if we are aware of the various levels on which revolution is taking place. In its loosest sense, all that we have been discussing in earlier chapters is revolutionary, indeed any search for salvation at all is revolutionary. As noted, it is the fact that we have failed or refused to take these appearances of revolution seriously enough that more physical, that is, more violent, revolutionary moves must appear. None of the other models for understanding what students are trying to do provides the opportunity to see the revolutionary impetus as real, but the model of the search for salvation offers an insight into student life, an insight that captures the finality with which ideals are today being pressed. "Revolution" then, as we see it, is a term that applies to many levels of student awareness and behavior that substantiate the behavior generally seen as revolutionary, chiefly tactical violence; but this insight should make it possible to realize the necessity of some other response than repression.

REVOLUTION AS ALIENATION AND OPPOSITION

The first level of revolution is the one which takes place in thinking. It is the revolution which has created among students, on so many issues, attitudes vastly different from those of adult society; such attitudes as those toward law, toward morality, toward authority. Alienation, I hold, is not so much a psychological condition of students as it is a conscious opposition to the rest of society; alienation is itself a revolution on this first level, the level of thinking. Clues to this revolution, and confirmation that it has already taken place, appear in all studies which attempt to discover the causes of present student attitudes, such as their having been the first television generation, the first generation raised permissively, the first affluent generation, and so on. Each of these points not so much to a cause as to a quiet revolution in the factors of which the individual personality is composed that has already taken place in our society, although the revolutionary qualities thus produced are unrecognized and unappreciated by most adults.

It is not only that students and other youth are different

from their predecessors but that they know they are different (as distinct from merely feeling it) and sense the power to press their difference openly. The revolution that has already taken place has produced aspirations and ideals for the social and political arena that as rhetoric are not new, but as realizable goals are more serious than they have been for some time. *Honesty* is perhaps the key concept, and the desire for openness and honesty, for bringing together whatever disparate tracks on which life is lived, for admitting fault and working for perfection, are simply traits of those already thus radicalized. Hypocrisy is the enemy, and certain kinds of muscular authority the enemy's tools.

The revolution that has already taken place provides much of the character of the search for salvation, since it is a revolution in thinking and attitudes. It is because of this revolution that the search for salvation has no meaning when it is thought of only in terms of traditional religious institutions or the irrelevantly constituted educational world. It does have meaning, if not fulfillment, when it is pressed in adventurous experiences such as with drugs, sensory awareness, or "different" religious disciplines. It is why the concern for an authentic individuality directed toward a humane sociality has gained such a strong appeal. The salvation sought must be authentically realizable and genuinely beneficial.

REVOLUTION FOR THE "HELL OF IT"

The second level of revolution is revolution for the hell of it, as Free calls it in *Revolution for the Hell of It*. ("Free" is thought to be a pseudonym for Abbie Hoffman.) This is the game model pressed to its furthest extent, including the renunciation of any seriousness whatever. It is, we might say, the indispensable element of humor which certain kinds of intellectuals thankfully bring to any movement. It reflects at once the hopelessness of serious revolution in this society and the necessity of untiring opposition to the world as it is. The revolution of complete noncooperation in a joyous and carefree spirit, it effectively exposes the arid sobriety with which the world sees itself. It is the revolution of the Youth International Party (the Yippies, who nominated a pig for President in 1968, and who treated their subsequent investigation by the House Committee on Un-American Activities as a costume ball). It is the incredibly inventive "Fuck the System" pamphlet, which swept New York City in the summer of 1968. This pamphlet, reproduced in full in *Revolution for the Hell of It*, describes how one can have life (and have it more abundantly) utterly free of charge in a big city, if one is willing to work night and day at the kind of noncooperation that refusing to earn money requires: free food, free phone calls, free college, free entertainment, free religion. In one sense, revolution for the hell of it exposes the colossal waste seemingly demanded by affluence and obsolescence. In another, it milks the system for all its spare benefits (and some not so spare). Morally, it is the fullest expression of the widespread belief in the young that to cheat an institution is not as serious as to violate the rights of another individual, and any business or government machine is fair game. This is a moral position which I have not seen effectively criticized. It cuts to the quick of our national hypocrisy that sees morality as primarily personal, rather than social, behavior. For an individual to steal from a corporation is as deadly wrong to the average moralist as for him to steal from another individual, or so he says. For a corporation to profit from its exploitations of the individual is a fact of life less accessible to moral judgment. The student who revolts just for the hell of it is testing out a precise reversal of this anomaly, for he demands morality on the social plane while denying its relevance in his personal affairs—always, "as long as nobody is hurt."

Revolution just for the hell of it is the revolution of the clown and the gadfly. Knowing that the system is so complex that nothing he can do will actually affect it, he satisfies himself simply by making its efficiency more difficult to maintain, and by aggravating it, making it less painful to himself. Since most of what he attacks in society is just that element of the world which takes itself with such great seriousness, and since his own mood is one of hit-and-run frivolity, he offers a salutary commentary of his own on the factors in our life which make salvation for the young so difficult. He also insists that the other levels of revolution should not take *them*selves too seriously.

Only those who think of comic relief as a luxury will miss the benefit of this kind of revolution in keeping hope alive on the other levels, and this is the function the Yippies have performed in their parodies of the New Left. That it is really revolutionary is no problem as witness the willingness of the policeman, the salesman, and the congressman alike to stamp it out whenever it appears. "To take nothing really seriously in American life!" There should never be a time when we are without such a conscience, costly as it may be to the individual who provides it. There can never be a viable revolution unless it is accompanied by another, just for the hell of it, which takes neither the *status quo* nor the pretensions of reformers as anything more than a bowl of cherries. On our model, of course, it is in itself a rejection of any possibility of salvation except in pure escape from the demands of a hostile world, not an altogether untraditional concept. If it continues to keep a sense of humor in the revolution, it will have its salvation, perhaps that of the juggler of Notre Dame.

The Yippies remind one, on reflection, of the disembodied chuckle that haunts Jean Baptiste Clamence in Camus's *The Fall*. Their effect on the society which cannot rid itself of them is the same as the effect of the haunting laughter on that character: a pursuing challenge of guilt to complacency, a charge of the essential sinfulness of the uptight.

REVOLUTION AS VIOLENCE AND DISRUPTION

The third level of revolution to be considered is the physical acts of violence and disruption with which we began this chapter. It is revolution as in Cuba, as philosophized in Marcuse. This level of revolution is desperate and serious in the extreme, with no room for the admission of error and no place for considered contemplation of consequences or alternatives. The point so far missed in commentary upon this level of revolution is what brings it on, which is the utter and complete failure of normal means of reform. In the American context, it has appeared several times since *the* Revolution, for example in abolitionism, in the development of the labor movement, and more recently in the black movement. In each case it has arisen only after a long period of relative failure in achieving demands felt to be rights of man, and in each case has been made possible by the moral indefensibility of the *status quo* against which the demands were made. As students have become revolutionary in this sense, it is partly in cooperation with the black revolution, and partly in reaction to the growing frustration with the failures of approved forms of activism to gain any attention to their rightful claim on their lives and destinies. This level of revolution requires a fine blend of anger and hope for success, both of which cut into the institutions of society at their most vulnerable point: impatience cuts into complacency, stridency into the capacity to talk a problem to death, noise into the quiet that is really escape from reality, and ingenuousness into the protections afforded by complexity. And weapons? Weapons, as already noted, prove that you expect to be heard.

The problems of physical revolution are as great as they are obvious. Most obvious of all is the fact that a revolution needs to succeed, and the revolution of blacks and students in America is, to say the least, highly unlikely to succeed. Nonviolence, undoubtedly, is the better tactic, if it can succeed in being incisive enough to draw the fire that the world levels on the true revolutionary, but this calls for ingenuity of an almost superhuman order. Precisely the reason that revolution is necessary is that our society has discovered its infinite capacity peacefully to absorb nonviolent protest. This means that the apocalyptic lure to value one's death in proportion to how great a havoc one can wreak in dying is very great. Apocalypse has already appeared on the campus; the task is to see that it ushers in a new world rather than confirming the old one in its power, as the invented apocalypse tends to do.

The other most pressing problem of revolution is its own inner failures, its own likelihood of producing tyrannies as great if not greater than those it replaces. This is perhaps peculiarly true for American revolutionaries, since the tyranny under which we live is systematic not personal, and is hence diffused throughout a variety of institutional forms. These institutions, to protect themselves, need only turn to other institutions for assistance, which they readily do, inasmuch as they recognize that it is institutionalism as such that is under attack. But the number and variety of institutions are such that no effective revolution of a physical kind can hope for success, only pointless bloodshed. In the event that revolution did prove successful in one kind of institution, the likelihood of a personal or oligarchical tyranny appearing would seem to be inevitable. Because of the diffusion of power, the temptation would be to aim revolution at the government, which is to say, to aim it away from the kind of power the revolution seeks to usurp: the power to sway the direction of institutional life away from institutionalism, away from structure, and toward a more humane and organic style.

Above all, physical revolution suffers from the diversity and spontaneity of the revolutionary impetus. The New Left and the radical students are simply not organized for revolution, only for spasmodic revolutionary activity. There is no capacity, even if radicalism were to win a revolutionary war, to fill the vacuum of power left by its initial successes. And this vacuum would undoubtedly then yield to the "revolutionaries" of the right. This is the truth implicit in the *caveat* leveled at students that the real danger they face is backlash—they so anger the general run of hardworking Americans that they will be irrationally opposed by them unless they cease antagonism. This caution too easily means that the students should accept the point of view of those who will lash back and is thus an advice impossible to accept. Somehow a revolutionary style that will stop just short of justifying such a backlash is needed, and is as yet wanting.

And yet, there is clearly a point of view from which the level of physical revolution must be seen as more than the fancies of a few of the more radical and politicized of students. Clearly, unless a bloodless revolution is midwifed into completion and breeds a genuine enthusiasm for the future in students, a bloody revolution is inevitable and will cost us our only hope of escape from mediocrity, banality, and the continuing hatred of the rest of the world. Most students tend to shy away from any serious talk of revolution as if it were the talk of a different kind of animal than they are, yet most students are also virtually bereft of hope that the society toward which they are growing is capable of real reform. They are *pre*revolutionaries, and for them, or for those armies of the young coming after them, revolution may in time become a more acceptable, because unavoidable, reality.

THE THREAT OF MORE REVOLUTION

At this point, with the threat of more physical revolution in the future, it might serve to observe the importance of anonymity in campus disruptions for most of the students. Leaders, of course, are not anonymous and take their lumps, but those who provide the numbers in a campus disruption act anonymously. Anonymity is their opportunity. But it may well also be their complaint. Especially where the type of student has known a kind of anonymity in his family life and finds it continued in college, knowing relief from anonymity only in the revolutionary community, the seeds of revolution are effectively sown. In the very small colleges, no one is anonymous, and misery, at least within the educational system, is less. In the large state universities, though the student may be anonymous on campus, it is likely that he is not from the kind of family where he has been anonymous since childhood, and again the misery is not as great. Large and complex institutions who draw their students from families where anonymity is a style of life have had the earliest and, as yet, the most serious disruptions. For in their students converges the anger to be justly directed at an inhumane society and the personal anger at not being dealt with on a personal level.

Physical revolution may be necessary simply because we are into a revolutionary time. It may require many more paroxysms in the black-white struggle before any kind of real humanity is recognized to exist in black skin, other than through outstanding ("qualified") individuals. As student alienation continues to be encouraged by the mistakes made in reaction to their attacks on the institution, and as the institution succeeds in preserving itself *qua* institution without regard for its vocation to be a community of education transcending anonymity and structure, the identification which students will feel with the "third world" and the revolutions that are economically and politically necessary elsewhere in the world (some of them made necessary by American policies) will develop in them a more clearly revolutionary stance toward their own society. Structures that will not yield to the insistent pressure of humane demand will be brought down by inhumane means. In the educational context, the response of teachers would seem to be decisive, and few have yet shown that they are willing to regard the students who refuse merely to emulate them as anything but potential enemies.

One specific response that would seem to be called for from teachers is the insistence that time be given periodically within the academic calendar for amply long and profoundly serious discussion on each campus of the proper role of the university in society. In a search for what Harvey Cox has called "the republic of virtue" as the *sine qua non* in the absence of which the "republic of intellect" is neutralized into uselessness, such discussion would serve well. This would be a mildly revolutionary tactic, if revolution involves the displacement of existing structures, since it would dislodge the tyranny of the routine calendar and the programed order of the teaching schedule. Moreover, it would require that teachers learn and students teach in many of the areas that would be discussed. Unstructured teach-ins have promoted a great deal of education over the years. The influence in society which the educational community might be able to effect might then be saving for all concerned. Until teachers use their ingenuity to show that they are allies in the revolution, the revolution will proceed in a form least consonant with real education.

More soberly, it seems to me that the rhetoric (and sometimes the acting out) of physical revolution will continue because it is necessary to keep the *possibility* of physical revolution alive until sufficient credence is given to admittedly virtuous aims of the revolutionaries. If those in control of the institutions that are the object of revolution are as fearful of substantive change as they have so far appeared to be, the possibility of physical revolution may be the only expression of real hope for change that gets heard.

It is not my aim to invest absolute hope in physical revolution, but to express as clearly as possible my feeling that it is in some circumstances inescapable. It is made necessary not by professional revolutionists, enamored of the mystique of Che Guevara, but by the unyielding response which the ideals of reform continue to encounter. Physical revolution is inevitable unless it is recognized that the search for salvation is a determined and demanding pressure on students. Salvation through revolution, unlikely though that be when the revolution is violent, is what is being sought, not revolution for its own sake or in the systematic interests of any traditional political alternatives.

REVOLUTION AS EXISTENTIAL COMMITMENT TO DECISIVE CHANGE

A fourth level of revolution is best thought of as an existential commitment to a decisive change in the roles which an individual will allow himself to fill in his life.

It is a kind of personal revolution, spiritual revolution if you like, involving deadly challenges to the *status quo* by its noncompliance in the traditional demands of its society. The revolutionary's commitment to kinds of work and styles of living which, as they emanate from him to others around him, will bring about social changes in a less direct manner than physical revolution, but with more permanent effect. This level of revolution has been experimented with in the hippie phenomenon, but that was only a trial run, a kind of rough draft. The symbol was hair, and the rhetoric was obscene, but both of these were merely external expressions of an interior change that is basic and reducible to no single manner of expression. The level of revolution as existential commitment is the internalization of the search for salvation, but it is emphatically not the escape into the self or into unconcern for the need for social change that it might appear to be. It is a kind of "going underground" politically, and it is most likely characterized by a calm, untroubled, even joyful No to the structures we have inherited and by a quiet, provisional, even wide-eyed Yes to possibilities of the future. It is not harmless, so I do not describe it to give relief to those who may fear other kinds of revolution. It is as full of potential for destruction of much we now hold dear as is suggested in Bob Dylan's old but haunting line about something happening without our knowing what it is. Its negative judgment is that the institutions we now have, in education, politics, law, religion, and the home, may be unredeemable.

The reason that other levels of revolution are important, apart from the fact of their dominance in our thought about students, is that any one of them or all of them may be routes to this fourth level of revolution. Other levels display the search for salvation being tested in ways that simply give expression to natural or traditional patterns of behavior: the revolution that has already taken place communicates itself to the young through the media of information and entertainment, revolution for the hell of it is an expression of the indispensable lightheartedness of youth, physical revolution is modeled on real revolutions of the past; each is an understandable response to known ways of pursuing one's grail, and each has the lure of the adventurously new, but each is new only in its locale or its specific content. The fourth level of revolution is new in form with each individual person, and new in effect, as each individual works out ways of gauging his effect on the world around him. Its character can be seen with the help of a novel already quoted, Ignazio Silone's *Bread and Wine*.

THE EXAMPLE OF PIETRO SPINA

Bread and Wine is the story of Pietro Spina, alias Don Paolo Spada, a revolutionary in the Italy of 1938, at the time of the conquest of Ethiopia. Against the dictatorship of the Fascist regime, Pietro has thrown in his lot with the Communists as the only hope of defeating the evil of the state. His alias is in the identity of a priest, a masquerade he takes on for security, in an irony of a high order since the church's complicity in the evil of the Fascist state is great—although Christianity, in Silone's view, is still capable of producing a real saint now and then. His development as a character includes two stages of classical revolutionary activity and a final stage that approximates the existential, fourth level of revolution under consideration. In the phase of activity in which he is occupied in the first section of the novel, Pietro displays all the elements of revolutionary practice; he has gone underground to solidify the portion of the organization for which he is responsible.

He is full of anti-Fascist rhetoric, unyielding and doctrinaire; he is idealistic about "the masses," in this case the peasants of the Abruzzi of his youth who suffer greatly from the bureaucratic complications of an efficient but oppressive state; he finds natural allies in the young; he participates in a loose but ubiquitous network of contacts, and maintains from his school days a hostility to the "realistic" sellout of those who, as noted in the earlier quote, live temporary lives.

This programmatic revolutionary campaign gives way under the pressure of the problems encountered in political revolution. Some of these are the necessity of constant flight from omniscient authorities, the self-interest of most of those he thought allies, the doctrinaire rigidity encountered. The disappointment he experiences in discovering the materialism of the peasants, that they will suffer under or rise up against any society only because that is what peasants are for and they will always be peasants, is a prelude for his more gloomy discovery of the chauvinism of the young who are stimulated by the war in Africa and the prospect of solving Italy's problems by increasing Ethiopia's. After a few acts of revolutionary despair and with the revolution crumbled at his feet, Pietro launches his private, existential revolution.

Pietro Spina's "fourth level" of revolution is intimated in an incident which occurs while he is masquerading as the priest, Don Paolo. He is lying sick in an inn and in his defenseless condition is importuned by an old woman who wants to make her confession. Such acts he had avoided successfully, since honor demanded limits on his imposture, but a natural compulsion to absolve and forgive grasped him. His generosity and understanding were dominical, and news of it spread widely and quickly. Soon he was so besieged with penitents that he had to flee. But the intimation is clear that his new revolution was to be an existential stance that would destroy inimical social structures (symbolized here in the church's "power" to absolve) simply as a result of his being who he was, a function of his placing himself just so in relation to others. Those who knew him would live changed lives, perhaps respond revolutionarily themselves to their situations. As he takes on his lone and private role as existential revolutionary, what he will do and where he will do it are not clear, and a program is not necessary. It is only necessary to resolve to be what he is, a priest of sorts (but not of the sort that is an officer of the past), a prophet. Apocalypse was avoided only because the revolution failed and that of which apocalyptic is a bastardization re-emerged, the revolutionary prophet.

Pietro's role is clarified in a breathtaking way when, to launch his new role, he calls on his old priest-teacher, whose maintenance of his own prophetic revolution has isolated him from church and society and left him bereft of any responsibilities, labeled as a dangerous man. Old Don Benedetto greets him with word of a conversation he has just had with one of Pietro's schoolmates, a doctor who had come grimly to announce to the teacher his decision to give up, to take a coveted bureaucratic medical post and silence his own yearnings for a prophetic role. In the name of realism, he has capitulated. The doctor had observed, so the old priest tells Pietro, that all is not lost since Pietro, even if alone of the schoolboys, has held on to his ideals. Don Benedetto even suggests that what Pietro pursues is a divine vocation when in response to the revolutionary's confession that he had lost his faith many years ago, he says, "In cases similar to yours it is just a silly mistake. . . . This would not be the first time that the Eternal Father felt obligated to hide Himself and take a pseudonym. As you know, He has never taken the [names] men have fastened on Him very seriously." In the spirit of such a blessing, the priest tells Pietro that the doctor had taken comfort from Pietro's continued idealism. " 'It is lucky that at least Pietro has been saved,' he had said. 'Saved?' said Pietro. 'Is there a past participle of save?' "

Is there a past participle of save? This is the question to which the existential revolutionary will never accept a systematic answer, for he identifies salvation as the extension to all men of the prophetic truth which compels him, and the full relation of all men to one another and to their environment, both social and natural. It is a task that can never be done, and this the political revolutionary never quite sees. Revolution as an existential decision requires the acceptance of salvation as an endless search and at the same time as firm a commitment to the search as any more reachable form of "salvation" might offer.

THE EXISTENTIAL REVOLUTIONARY AND THE FUTURE

The existential revolutionary, like Pietro Spina, begins by the inward act of refusing to cast himself in the roles that are provided for him. He will not act in expected and predictable ways, *not even as a revolutionary*. His first act is saying NO: "In every dictatorship, just one man, even any little man at all, who continues to think with his own head puts the whole public order in danger. Tons of printed paper propagate the regime's order of the day, thousands of loudspeakers, hundreds of thousands of posters, and handbills distributed free, and stables of orators in the squares and crossroads, thousands of priests from the pulpit, all repeat to the point of obsession, to the point of collective stupefaction, these orders of the day. But it's enough that a little man, just one little man says NO for all that formidable granite order to be in danger." *

American society is not a dictatorship, and no college or university is likely to be a dictatorship for long, because of the diffusion of power that characterizes our system. This means that in our society it will take more than "just one little man" to make this kind of revolution. It might take, however, "just one little minority," and this is the power that a minority can have in America. And not just for the hell of it, but because the profferings and benefits of the system are rejected out of hand as costing too much in pain and poverty for those excluded. Both in the activism of *not doing* and in that of *doing,* the prophetic revolutionary will work out his program. Few will be as Christlike as Pietro Spina. But this kind of revolution will, nonviolently, put any self-protective establishment up against the wall. It is also a revolution not reserved to any age or race—only to those who can realize that as long as there are victims held down by our structures, it is they who must feel victimized; and in so identifying themselves—*authentically* because of their own existential decision—they participate in the salvation of others while pressing the search for their own.

Some examples come to mind. The young college graduate who is against the draft for reasons as moral and as substantial as any conscientious objector or guileless pacifist, but who has discovered that the easiest route is to teach school and try to get a II-S classification for an essential occupation. He accepts himself as he is, and his program is only to try to be himself wherever he can, a choice still within the realm of his own deciding. His effect on the school in which he teaches, on its curriculum, on its humanity, on its direction, can be immense, precisely because

* Ignazio Silone, *Bread and Wine* (New York: Atheneum, 1962), p. 216. Used with permission.

he is not "qualified" by training in education to be a teacher. He is not fitting into any role provided for him by the structures of education, and the possibility is open to him precisely because those structures have stopped working in lots of school systems. He is a revolutionary.

The Peace Corps attracted many college-age people and appealed to their idealism and interest in the non-American world. Thrown into situations which had little to do with any of the structured roles for which growing up in America had prepared them, many found that their own capacity for decision and commitment gave meaning to the technical preparation given them by the Corps. They found out in the Peace Corps that they could be educated pretty effectively to do all sorts of things for which college had not educated them, that college-as-training is not worth the time it takes in our accepted structures. More significantly, many of them returned in a condition unable to accept the complacency and self-righteousness of American life ever again. These found themselves existential revolutionaries.

Not a few Vietnam veterans were converted to an existential revolution by their experience of the American program in Southeast Asia, and will not again easily accept the role they might have fallen into had they merely accepted the standard Good Samaritanism of military interpretations of American policy. Whatever they do, it will not be predictable or traditional. Their roles will be of their own creation.

There are many student revolutionaries of this kind who simply do not plan to do the kind of work they will be expected to do, live in the kind of neighborhood they will be expected to, or perpetuate the kind of rituals of family and community existence expected of them. They are learning, on the other levels of revolution, the necessity for change; inside them, many are learning the reality of the search for salvation, that it is really pursued in a revolutionary loneliness of personal commitment to be what they are and to become what they are to become—not to fit into someone else's conception of what they are. Some may not get married; some who do may not have children; some may not ever work for anyone else; some in professions may eschew all the rewards associated with the profession in order to serve those in need. To take only one example, the future of that social institution known as the American Medical Association may be quite exciting when the prophetic revolutionaries in that field begin to discover each other at future meetings. Catch-22 is that "they will do whatever you let them do." The revolution that is serious and that can succeed is that of those who have decided to stop letting them do it. This revolution will be an even greater affront to those who earnestly desire what more and more students are rejecting than a violent revolution would be, and I suspect it is this lack of concern for what Americans have long striven for—security and status and prosperity, without soul—that makes America so angry at students. And the only point of campus disruptions is that it makes everyone face the fact that the rejection is taking place. It behooves the educational institutions to examine this rejection closely and to decide whether, in the future, they wish to have the participation of the most articulate, the most sensitive, and the most adventurous—in other words, whether education is to be saved.

8

SAVED IN TIME

Work out your own salvation . . .
—Paul the Apostle

It has been our thesis that the model for understanding the campus apocalypse that best draws together the variety of activities in which students are involved is the religious model of the search for salvation. For the inward looking activities of drug use and sensitivity explorations, and for the fascination with the unusual in religions, the clearest explanation is that students are seeking to know themselves and one another as fully as possible, and to discover what it might be that unifies and brings together the disparate experiences of the young human being. They have turned to these things because more traditional patterns of growth and fulfillment afford little self-knowledge and tend to fragment rather than unite people, and because the institutions in which traditional paths to salvation are preserved have lost the seriousness of purpose that is required. For the most part, institutions concerned with growing up—church, school, family—have turned in upon themselves for self-preservation and have diminished thereby the sense of their own purpose. What these institutions have traditionally communicated to rising generations, students still want, but they feel that they have to seek it elsewhere.

140

But the search for salvation is not confined to the quest for inner peace and self-knowledge. It looks outward also to the social and communal factors which impede salvation, and seeks to correct or displace those impediments in the interest of the proper balance between one's own hope for individual salvation and the possibility of salvation for others. Here, too, the institutions of society which exist for the purpose of assisting the individual in his efforts to establish saving relationships in the communities in which he lives have, in the eyes of students, become part of the problem rather than agents for its solution. It is an altogether salutary insight that no salvation is possible unless these corporate expressions of human community are changed, their structures made subservient to their responsibility to humanity rather than allowed to continue to serve abstract ideals or worse the security and profit of only a few. One of the keys to the outward-looking, activist, and revolutionary dimension of the search for salvation is the students' sense of identification with humanity, which extends beyond boundaries long cherished, boundaries which they find artificial and arbitrary: the boundaries of age, race, status, and nation. It may prove impossible to erase these boundaries in any effective way without creating other more dangerous boundaries in the process. An example is the frightful moral polarization that has already been described. Students should hold to their present course without losing their gift for hilarity as they drive toward securing power for change, and at the least should spend great effort in self-examination in order to avoid the insidious capacity of hypocrisy to chew away at their candor and openness, of which the first sign is taking themselves too seriously. This means that students should realize (as much as the rest of society should realize) that it is something like a search for salvation that they are involved in.

How Salvation Should Not Be Interpreted

The model will not be useful to either students or anyone else unless several aspects of its construction are clearly understood. With anything that smacks of religion, we must be most careful because of the shoddy and irresponsible attitudes marketed in the name of religion. For one thing, the model is not used for the purpose of relieving our present situation of any of its tension. Of such character is American religion that we are capable of writing off as essentially unimportant anything that is connected with it. Many Americans, religious and antireligious as far as their relation to existing churches and sects is concerned, will err in thinking that students will grow out of the search for salvation into "realism" or "maturity" in time. Some might even use the model to belittle campus unrest as frivolous. They err gravely, and only show their shallowness. The overpowering demand for meaning and purpose which the search for salvation implies may grasp these people someday. But as long as their feeling is that there is nothing that would bear the name "salvation" that could possibly occupy serious minds, they show their fundamental misunderstanding of the model, and of religion, whatever their own religious label. One of the things the model suggests, to which we shall return, is that religion as we have known it is in for some decisive changes, some of which have already appeared. Particularly, a fresh approach to the vocabulary used in religious talk will be required.

The model also is not intended to reduce the turmoil of campus life today to the strictures of any particular definition of salvation possessed by any religious or philosophical stance. The danger of this is serious enough that I wish there were another word than "salvation" to use since most readers, again whether they are themselves members of any religious community or not, probably have a definition of salvation in mind which they will be tempted to apply to this discussion in order to handle it. They may have one of two purposes or desires in mind in doing this. First, some may wish to go along with student idealism to a certain point, then draw the line beyond which they will not agree to the continuation of the search for salvation because salvation as they know it cannot be activist or revolutionary or violent. They may wish to bring a particular definition of salvation as interior, rather than exterior, activity to bear on the issue in order to rule out the possibility of activism (and relevance) altogether. More crudely they may be forced by the traditions which hold them to define salvation as referring to some entirely otherworldly existence awaiting them (and their children) after death. Whatever hold this doctrine has had on religious people in the Western world in the past, the secularism of recent centuries has completely destroyed it, and its destruction constitutes a liberation of the human spirit from severe restrictions. Organized religion bears a grave responsibility for attempting to keep alive an otherworldly doctrine of salvation that allows a sense of helplessness about the evil in this world to prevail. Any black Christian can testify to one of the more insidious uses to which such a doctrine has been put. If it requires a sloganistic approach to make clear that the God of this doctrine is dead, then so be it. Meanwhile, fewer and fewer students see the doctrine as any more than a distraction from the salvific task at hand, that of laying hold in this life on a work that holds ultimate meaning for them. The force of ultimacy is not to defer the goal to an improbable future, but to inspire fidelity in constructing the future.

Second, others may wish to impose a particular definition of salvation upon the model in order, in the name of dying religion, to exploit the energy and exuberance of youth so that new life can be breathed into the churches. A premature identification on the part of religious people with the students' search for salvation which entertains the illusion that students are really after the same things the religious institutions are after is in for a disappointment. A valiant effort was made by the University Christian Movement to relate the official church bodies of the National Council of Churches to the students' search for salvation, but fortunately the students' understanding prevailed and, perhaps unique among church agencies, the UCM has gone voluntarily out of existence. The reason is that what students were doing was not capable of being related to what the institutional churches were doing, chiefly because the alliances among students in their causes have no relation to the artificial religious boundaries tolerated in the pan-Protestant religious establishment. To pretend that a church-based movement could maintain relation with what students were actually doing, in all its variety and all its iconoclasm, was, fortunately, recognized as only possible if it were some kind of exploitation of student organizations by the churches. The facts indicate that the structures that already exist cannot be adapted to include students, even those who may still find some reason to call themselves Christians. For one thing, the students involved are more closely associated with their Jewish and pagan fellow students than they are with their elder brothers in the churches.

The Value of the Salvation Concept

The value of the religious model of the search for salvation is precisely that it resists either of these tendencies to confine it to a particular course of action or a particular direction merely by the application of an approved definition of salvation to it. Salvation is the one religious theme that is clearly future oriented, and the only way to structure it so as to make it conform to established experience is to relegate it to an afterlife and remove its pressure from this one. Once that is grown out of, the search for salvation is like the Spirit in the Gospel of John, "it blows where it will."

Is, then, the salvation experience any kind of usable model? I think it is if it is remembered that the usefulness of a model is dependent on its capacity to give some insight into experienced phenomena otherwise unexplained without interfering with the character of the phenomena. The model is useful only if it is itself correctable, as experience grows, without needing to be replaced. The religious model, rather than the therapy, game, or generational models, leaves free the course of action which student life will take for further choices while at the same time recognizing that what that course of action is concerned with is serious and purposeful, rather than frivolous or merely destructive of institutions for the sake of destruction. If it is true that there is no "past participle of save," the provisional structure of the model and its resistance to the application of dogmatic definitions of salvation is assured.

Another misuse of the model occurs when the reaction to the discovery that students are in search of salvation is that they should do it on their own time, that the problems of the society and the setting of the university are unfit places for the search to take place. I have already indicated that on its own terms the educational establishment offers itself as a kind of salvation to students, and I think it has come to do so because it can use no less a goal to verify its own seriousness and sense of purpose. If this is so, then the issue becomes the manner of its offering and the success of its communication of its purpose to students, and this is precisely where the present conflict in the university itself arises. The problem of relevance is central here, and the demand of students for participation in decisions about the manner in which the educational community pursues its purpose and about the kind of life it engenders while doing so is a just demand.

There might well be student resistance to the use of the religious model on the grounds that it might seem to students to contain a hidden agenda implying the accreditation of religion when, as indeed has been argued, their critique of received religion is severe and irreversible. They might argue that the areas of student activity we have described are in fact activities taken up for their own sake. This might be particularly compelling in the evaluation of activism and revolution, which are, to students and many others including the writer, self-evidently necessary and require no ulterior justification. Again the character of the salvation model secures the necessary freedom of motive without allowing what many adults think is the aimless and purposeless quality of student unrest. I have defended students in their lack of "alternatives" on the grounds that negative action might be as much as can be expected when there is so much to be negative about. Positive constructions will appear when radical victories begin decisively to occur. They will, of course, be extremely difficult to achieve, and the results may in turn require radical criticism at a future time. But there is no justification for assuming that absence of alternative programs charting a life on the other side of yet undestroyed barriers means inability to devise programs when the time comes. This defense against the criticism of radical students most confidently levelled by their opponents arises from the validity of the model being used here. There is nothing ulterior implied in labeling activism saving. The salvation sought, and the salvation to be realized, are not different from, nor posterior to, the success of the activist program itself. The only additional note it adds which is not always present in activism as such is the necessity for endurance, for not succumbing to the temptation to think the millennium has arrived, for not giving in too easily. Salvation is another, perhaps more important, name for what students are seeking under a variety of headings. It draws the various activities together without dogmatizing about what the final goal will look like.

A valid analysis is long overdue of the music of the revolution. At least as much effort ought to be expended on getting to know it as on any other aspect of student life. It affords, moreover, a precise example of the subtle importance of the religious model as a confirmation of the seriousness of all we have been discussing. In a recent article, Michael Lydon ("Rock for Sale," *Ramparts,* June 1969) explored the ambiguity of the relationship between rock music and the revolution, and how "rock, rather than being an example of how freedom can be achieved within the capitalist structure, is an example of how capitalism can, almost without a conscious effort, deceive those whom it oppresses." This would be sufficient evidence of the necessary failure of all levels of revolution as earlier described, were it not for the fact that there are exceptions, like the Grateful Dead, who maintain "we won't play bad music for the bread because we decided a long time ago that money wasn't a high enough value to sacrifice anything for." (Quoted by Michael Lydon in his article.) They are badly in debt because they do not play the establishment commercial game. There are others, by definition unknown, following the same ideal, but also there are countless amateur musicians purveying the revolution entirely outside the commercial structure. They can sell out to the record companies and "plunder American society for enough money to escape it," or they can have some confidence that their intuitions are to be taken seriously and the lure resisted. The salvation model, without offering any ulterior rewards, but only the rewards identical with the goals of the search under its other labels, might provide this confidence, as well as bring together the varieties of revolutionary experience into the manifest unity of aspiration to which we have pointed as this discussion has developed.

THE STUDENT THEOLOGY OF SALVATION

Within the framework of this unity of aspiration, it can be seen what is rejected and what affirmed in the search for salvation, or, to put it another way, what "theology of salvation" is being worked out by students in their revolutionary activity. The most general proposition to be discerned is a recovery of the identity of a developing humanity with an unfolding salvation. To be saved in time requires bringing together salvation and humanity, a pairing of concepts so continuously elusive in human experience and so remarkable whenever it appears that it will be a mistake of the most serious kind to destroy it in the interests of preserving institutions or in the service of some shibboleth of traditional loyalties. In the theological world, saved *and* human is the proper description for the recent developments in theological thinking from Kierkegaard and Buber to Teilhard de Chardin. Increasingly, theology has recognized the necessity of speaking with temporal pertinence, which is to say, to humanity as it is lived.

To attempt to bring together saved *and* human, or the search for salvation and the integrity of the human experience, is to reject completely any suggestions that the quest for meaning and purpose is to be deferred to a future time that will be brought into being by the mere march of time and progress. Hence it is to find useless any advice to be patient. The complexity of human relationships and the necessity for detailed negotiation on issues to arrive at agreement among interested people are not denied by campus activists, let alone beyond their comprehension. The advice they reject is that they be patient while others, or time itself, or the playing out of systems arrive at the humane conclusion desired. This is the familiar demand to participate in decision making, to be included in the difficulty, and to be allowed to evaluate the factors which complicate institutional life. The very demand thus defines institutions as comprising *all* the human elements affected by their works, not just those who pay for them or profit from them. To be denied such participation is to have one's humanity denigrated, and hence to be damned. To oppose the force which denies such participation is to assert one's humanity and at the same time to assert one's right not to be damned by someone else, the right to seek a salvation.

To bring together salvation and humanity requires that students do everything they can to be delivered from perpetuating the world as it is or accepting life as static and determined. Their frequent analysis that their elders have rejected their own experience in order to comply with some authority to which they have subjected themselves points at one time both to the inauthenticity of experience as it is communicated to them and to the evil of certain kinds of authority. Instead of imitating the pattern, they explore the nuances of personal experience with the help of any means available and do so without regard to the authority that fails to show any right to its position. They refuse any pattern of human existence which excludes other than by genuine choice this or that kind of experience for fear that only a truncated humanity will result. And a truncated humanity produces a society in which no salvation is possible.

Thus there can be no salvation when human concerns are deferred for the sake of property or institutional needs.

When some (in fact many) are in such great need of relief from the structures which perpetuate their inhuman existence, the material and spiritual blessings which the structures provide for others are without attraction for concerned students. To be human is to recognize one's indispensable relation to all who, but for oneself, might also be fully human. Thus to be saved from the collective guilt of participation in a society which has become idolatrous about law, insensitive to its supportive constituents, religiously trivial, and helpless in the face of war, racial dishonor, and poverty requires expressing that relation to others not yet fully human as a result. Paul Goodman has observed that pacifism is essentially revolutionary. So also are sacrifice, identification with the oppressed, and most forms of intense human mutuality. The values that the settled society recognizes in its rhetoric, no matter how firmly possessed in the face of the demands of those who do not possess them, are simply not saving if they exist at the expense of another's human growth and enrichment. This goal is hopelessly egalitarian in a world still controlled by an animal hierarchy of power and privilege. The significant note of the campus rebellion, and it is this which makes it so inimical to the established powers, is that those most likely to be the powers of the next generation and to enjoy the privileges of the undisturbed continuance of things as they are, are rejecting, in the name of a simple humanity and a not-so-simple insistence on the identification of humanity and salvation, the very opportunities they inherit.

The proper response to the recognition of the seriousness of the search for salvation is to join it. By this is meant that the student search is too serious and hopeful, however erratic in details, to be abandoned. It will continue. The adult society, with notable exceptions, seems to have decided that student radicalism must be put down as an alien and barbaric threat. The polarization that results is already dangerous, and when it is complete the *apocalyptic* attitude appears on both sides. Such an attitude is made necessary when our confidence in the present and the near future wanes, when we decide that it is necessary to make things that are happening stop happening. Religiously, the apocalyptic temper appears when confidence in being able to work out our salvation vanishes. Only God, so religious apocalyptists believe, can right the situation and in doing so he will vindicate "us" and destroy "them." Religious apocalyptists have always been able to trust that if this world were destroyed in the process, a new heaven and a new earth could result. In the secular age, apocalypticism is acceptance of suicide, and fear of the young and coming generation is probably its first sign. But the threat of apocalypticism can also implement the consciousness of change which is required for any hopeful acceptance of the future of man. Change is not itself a virtue, but suspicion of it is always a vice. The society that demands the destruction of its most hopeful sources of change renounces its humanity. For when seeking salvation, humanity is not a static entity from which to escape, but a process to direct. Thus, to be saved in time is to recognize that none of our accepted values have any meaning if they fail to include the developing human community. The search for salvation is urgent, for the desired future must be brought into the inadequate present before the future disappears. This is precisely what students in such activities as we have been discussing are trying to achieve. True, they can be destroyed or at least silenced. But the cost of either is also the loss of our salvation.

SELECTED READINGS

1 WHAT ARE STUDENTS TRYING TO DO?

Butz, Otto, ed., *To Make a Difference*. New York, Harper & Row, 1967.

Keniston, Kenneth, *The Young Radicals*. New York, Harcourt, Brace & World, 1968.

2 THE LURE OF DRUGS

Braden, William, *The Private Sea: LSD and the Search for God*. Chicago, Quadrangle, 1967.

Cohen, Sidney, *The Beyond Within: The LSD Story*. New York, Atheneum, 1964.

Farina, Richard, *Been Down So Long It Looks Like Up to Me*. New York, Random House, 1966.

Matthiessen, Peter, *At Play in the Fields of the Lord*. New York, Random House, 1965. Also a Signet paperback.

3 THE PROMISE SOUGHT IN SENSITIVITY TRAINING

Buber, Martin, *I and Thou*. New York, Charles Scribner's Sons, 1958, 2nd ed. (This book is, of course, about the fact, not the technique.)

4 SEARCHING AMONG THE RELIGIONS

Gibran, Kahlil, *The Prophet*. New York, Alfred A. Knopf, 1923.

Merton, Thomas, *Mystics and Zen Masters*. New York, Farrar, Straus & Giroux, 1967.

Watts, Alan W., *The Joyous Cosmology*. New York, Pantheon, 1962. Also a Vintage paperback.

5   SAVING ACTIVISM

Jacobs, Paul, and Landau, Saul, *The New Radicals: A Report with Documents*. New York, Random House, 1966. Also a Vintage paperback.

Marcuse, Herbert, *One Dimensional Man*. Boston, Beacon, 1964.

Rights in Conflict ("The Walker Report"). New York, Bantam, 1969.

"Students and Politics," *Daedalus,* Winter, 1968.

6   INTERLUDE ON RELEVANCE: ITS INDISPENSABILITY

Grier, W. H., and Cobbs, P. M., *Black Rage*. New York, Basic Books, 1968. Also a Bantam paperback.

Heller, Joseph, *Catch-22*. New York, Simon & Schuster, 1961.

Watts, Alan, *The Book: On the Taboo Against Knowing Who You Are*. New York, Pantheon, 1966.

(I should like to add that the film If. . . is very illuminating.)

7   SALVATION THROUGH REVOLUTION

The Berkeley Barb

Cleaver, Eldridge, *Soul on Ice*. New York, McGraw-Hill, 1968. Also a Dell paperback, 1969.

Free, *Revolution for the Hell of It*. New York, Dial, 1968.

Kunen, J. S., *The Strawberry Statement*. New York, Random House, 1969.

Rader, Dotson, *I Ain't Marchin' Anymore!* New York, David McKay, 1969.

Silone, Ignazio, *Bread and Wine*. New York, Atheneum, 1962. Also a Signet paperback.

8   SAVED IN TIME

Moltmann, Jürgen, *Religion, Revolution, and the Future*. New York, Charles Scribner's Sons, 1969.

Novak, Michael, *Theology for Radical Politics.* New York, Herder & Herder, 1969.

Teilhard de Chardin, Pierre, *Hymn of the Universe.* New York, Harper & Row, 1965.